The
Jordanians
and the People of the Jordan

The
Jordanians

and the People of the Jordan

Dr. Kamel S. Abu Jaber

HESPERUS

Published by Hesperus Press Limited
www.hesperus.press

First Edition Published by Royal Scientific Society, 1980
Second Edition Published by Hesperus Press Limited, 2021

Designed and typeset by Roland Codd

Printed in the United Kingdom

ISBN 978-1-84391-987-2
ebook ISBN 978-1-84391-988-9

To my beloved,
The jordanians,
The palestinians,
The people of the Jordan.

Contents

Foreword

If you wish to read a book about Jordan and its people that is written in the words and language of a poet, who is also an intellectual leader, a first rate diplomat, and an outstanding scholar who truly loved his country, then this is your book, authored by the late Dr. Kamel Abu Jaber, may he rest in peace. It is a book that spans the modern past of Jordan, tells its stories, provides difficult to obtain data, and analyses Jordan's birth, development, styles of governance, family life, past and incumbent customs and cultures, the arts, and the challenges. The book reconciles the vintage with the modern in a story-like setting, describes what is and what can be, and integrates best practice with the local story that only a native son knows and appreciates, and tells it with an encompassing and inclusive voice of all Jordanians. Beware, however, this is not a sojourn into the world of academia, it is far beyond that; this book is a love psalm! A love story between a country and his people … One that is told by the forever articulate and devoted to Jordan and its people, Dr. Kamel Abu Jaber

Dr. Yusuf Mansur, 2021

Arches of Hope, coffee on paper, Suheil Bisharat, 1979.

Introduction

My husband wrote this book in the 1970s when he was dean of the college of economics and commerce at the University of Jordan. He wrote this in an effort to explain the thoughts feelings and aspirations of the Jordanians, Palestinians, and Arabs, whom he felt were mistreated and often misunderstood by the Western world, to provide insight into who we really are. It also serves to remind the youth of today and older generations of who they are and of their magnificent cultural heritage.

He was proud of his beloved country's progress and development in keeping up with the changing world, and felt that while he was looking older with more gray hair and wrinkles, Jordan kept looking younger and more vibrant . In this second edition, republished on the occasion of the 100th anniversary of the establishment of Jordan, I have added new statistical data for 2020 to illustrate the country's fantastic development and achievements since 1980, in spite of its many challenges.

Loretta Pacifico Abu Jaber, 2021

Acknowledgements

This labor of love would not have been possible without the encouragement and enthusiastic support of my children and grandchildren and the gracious assistance of my dear friend Ica Wahabeh, former managing editor, editor of the opinion page of the Jordan Times *Newspaper.*

Heartfelt thanks to the estate of our long time and dear friend, prominent Jordanian artist, the late Mohanna Durra, (1938–2021), cultural icon, ardent advocate for art education in the kingdom. He established the Fine Arts section of the Department of Culture and Art, and the Jourdan Institute of Fine Arts. His painting of a Bedouin graces the book's cover.

Additionally, I would like to extend thanks to our good friends, Jordanian artists Suhail Bisharat for his painting, Arches of Hope, *coffee on paper,1979; and Riham Ghassib,* Amman, *acrylic on canvas, 1994.*

Thanks to Kelvin Brown for newly restored pictures of Jordan during the early 20th century.

A sincere thanks to Dr. Yusuf Mansour, economist, former Minister os State for Economic Affairs for writing a Foreword to the book.

On behalf of myself and my late husband who was recently, posthumously, awarded the State Centennial Medal for service to his country, I would like to take this opportunity to congratulate his Majesty King Abdullah the Second, the Hashemite kingdom of Jordan and the people of Jordan on the Centennial of our beloved country. Alf mabrook.

Preface

The information in these personal essays is as accurate as humanly possible. Statistics and/or citations, whenever and wherever they appear, are there to illustrate a point, to clarify an issue, to generate interest and to elucidate feelings. These essays contain my inner thoughts, opinions, emotions, and feelings about who we are, and about the myriad issues that confront us. I have attempted to articulate to the non-Arab reader my and my people's — Jordanian Arabs — sentiments and thoughts. I was prompted to do so by my feeling that we are misunderstood, and this, in turn, because we often behave in an illogical and contradictory manner. In our frustration and anger, we have lost the ability to communicate clearly with others. These essays express the thoughts of a people — the Jordanians, Palestinians, Arabs — unjustly treated and often deliberately misunderstood. I do hope they will give the reader an insight into who we are.

Ferry boat on the River Jordan, 1934–39.
G. Eric and Edith Matson, American Colony (Jerusalem).
Photo Department. Library of Congress.
Restoration by Kelvin Bown. *Reawakening the Past*, 2015.

Chapter One

The Jordan and the People of Jordan

The Jordan is only a river that runs in the deepest gorge on the face of this earth. Meandering from north to south through the Great Rift Valley that continues down to East Africa, the Jordan River pours into the Dead Sea, almost 400 meters below sea level. The Dead Sea, and the harsh and severe surrounding hills, is one of the strangest, yet most beautiful and eeriest places on earth. In most of the area, it is as if one suddenly found oneself on the surface of the moon, Mars, or some other far-flung planet. This is especially true late at night and in the summer.

Though it is only a river, a natural phenomenon whose waters touch both banks, in recent decades it has become a dividing line, a boundary separating the Hashemite Kingdom of Jordan from Palestine ... the East from the West Bank. It has become a meeting place and a separation line. The Jordan Valley, a huge, elongated bowl, hugs the hills of both Palestine and Jordan, forming on both sides an escarpment of unusually beautiful proportions, deep, dangerous, and often breathtaking. It is much harsher on the West Bank, where it is also steeper and saltier. The off-white color of its earth gives the atmosphere a certain unreal quality that is hard to find anywhere else. Around Jericho, or Deir Mar Saba, one feels close to nature and to God, feels the magnificence of God's creation and the insignificant nature of man's existence.

The River: Source of Life

The Jordanians? Who are they? I shall come to that in good time. The land has had something to do with the people and has influenced their character. Surely, the Jordan River is only a body of water forming the western boundary of the country Jordan. But it is not just another river. In fact, by the standards of respectable international rivers or riverine basins like the Nile, Amazon, Mississippi, Yellow River, or Ganges, it is not a river at all. Today it is only a trickle, and one has to conjure up all sorts of powers of imagination to elicit the image of a river. Since 1948, the Israeli authorities have changed the shape of the land, diverted much of its waters, and dried up lake Hula. Much history and much romance and sanctity were sacrificed to raise tomatoes and vegetables to feed the Jewish immigrants who flocked into Palestine. But that is politics, and that will be discussed elsewhere.

Let us consider the river, the source of life and inspiration. John the Baptist drank from its waters. He came out of the Jordanian desert, no doubt looking wild and having eaten locusts and wild honey, and settled by its eastern bank. Imagine that bushy-bearded, romantic, gentle, clairvoyant, and inspired personality, John the Baptist, in Arabic called Prophet *Yahya*, thundering his prophecies some 2,000 years ago. I often wonder to whom he could have been prophesying in the Jordanian desert in those days, for he is described as having come out of the wilderness. John, *Yahya*, son of Zachariah, had one of the greatest honors of all times, an honor that God bestowed upon him at least three times: once, by choosing him as a prophet; secondly, by having him predict one of the greatest dramas of human existence, the coming of Jesus, in Arabic *Issa Ibn Mariam*, son of Mary; and thirdly, by having him baptize the Prophet Jesus in the waters ever since then known as the waters of the holy River Jordan. Other names the people of Palestine and Jordan call their river are *Al-Shari'ah*, the *Mawrid*, the source, the straight path, the ford, a place where people used to cross from one side to another. An old wooden bridge on the river survived until 1918, when it was destroyed by the retreating Turks. Later, it was rebuilt as a steel structure and called the Allenby Bridge. Now it is called the King Hussein Bridge.

In several other locations, however, people wishing to cross had either to swim, ford it or be transported on the backs of men who had made a livelihood out of carrying people across. At one spot, some say, there was also a primitive raft that used to cross the river by means of ropes and pulleys. This raft could not be operated in the winter when the river flooded.

For, until well into the 1930s, the river and the surrounding gorge were still in a natural state. The river still flooded, and wild beasts still lived on its eastern banks. I was told that wild boar, deer, and even tigers and leopards used to be hunted there. Bedouin lore and poetry speak of the existence of lions near Zarka, and I have heard some Bedouins speak of *Masba'at al Zarka*, the lion-den in Zarka. One Bedouin poet, possibly Nimr al-Adwan, most famous of Jordan's Bedouin poets, says in one verse: "I looked up … and saw the one with the spotted body (the leopard) … and I said (to myself) life is finished and death is near!"

But death is always near in the Middle East; but then, so is life. The river Jordan is now only a trickle, further degraded by a continual flood of tourists who are shocked by what is left of it, but inspired by the *barakah*, the blessing of being near it and happy to be able to dip their hands in its now saline waters. One wonders if raising tomatoes and other vegetables in the Negev area is an appropriate price. One wonder, why there should be a price and why no one on the face of this earth does something to maintain and keep its sanctity. Tourist agencies have now organized tours, and some bottle the saline water in small vials and sell it to the boastful, the religious or the romantic. The degradation of the river in this century has no equal in previous times. In the old days, thank God, men did not have the technology to move mountains or to dam and divert rivers on the scale of modern times. It is doubly sad, since the degradation was done by a people so aware of history … they themselves its product, its victim and its creator.

Echoes- of the land

That is the river, the source of life that gave the land its name: *Al-Urdun*, Jordan. A land as old as time. It is here, some say, that man first appeared about 200,000 years ago. The pre and post Neanderthal; Homo sapiens, with agricultural settlements, mud abodes, small villages, larger towns, always surrounded by walls. Man, it seems, always needed protection from himself. Remember when the walls of Jericho came tumbling down? The Jordan Valley is full of such settlements, with Tel al-Ghassoul one of the most recently discovered.

There is hardly a *tel*, mountain, or a *wadi*, valley, that has not been tread upon by a prophet, or at least some important, venerable leader, and often a tyrant. Moses, *Musa, Kalim Allah*, the one who was given the honor of speaking with God, was lost for 40 years in the *Tih*, the wilderness of Sinai, in south Palestine and south Jordan. And then, when the Lord guided his steps, his people's sheep and goats grazed the Sharah mountains in south Jordan and proceeded further north until they reached Siyaghah, Mount Nebo, near present day Madaba. From there he was only to look at the land of milk and honey … Palestine … only to look, but not to lead his people into it. That honor was accorded to his brother Aaron, *Harun*, and his captains. Whenever I visit that area and look from the same spot westwards towards Palestine, I wonder how *Sayyidnah Musa*, our Master Moses, felt having only to look … what a terrible punishment after at least 40 years of wandering. The gentle and the cruel have always coexisted, and it is here in Jordan that dreams of the coexistence of the wolf and the lamb are made.

Too much history in this land, a land haunted by the echoes of history … pre-Biblical, Biblical, Hellenistic, Roman, Islamic, and now modern times. It is too intense, ever-present, and permeating. How can one forget it, with every *tel*, indeed, every landmark denoting some significant biblical event? Too much enmity, love, blood, tears and sweat where the shape and the course of humanity was influenced. The shadow of history is always here, elongated beyond belief, giving further dimensions to the land and its people. Even the humblest Bedouin, villager or townsman can recount some historical events, embellishing them with the spice of life, their own interpretation. Once I listened to an old man talking, and in the course of his talk he casually mentioned how he saw Ibrahim Pasha in Salt. Salt is one of the most beautiful towns of central Jordan; it used to be an important outpost of government in Ottoman times. Ibrahim Pasha, son of Mohammad Ali (1805–1848), the founder of modern Egypt, was in Salt in the early 1830s, and our speaker was no more than 65 or 70 years old. It just could not be, but then the man was not a liar. In his mind, he was telling the truth; for in his mind's eye, myth and reality had merged, as they often do in the Levant. So much history and so much pain, humanity, and suffering. It has shaped us so that every Jordanian, indeed almost every Arab, is a poet who gets thrilled, gets high on the language that carries so much meaning and so much history.

Sometimes I think we should ban our history from being taught in schools. There is too much discrepancy between what was and what is. To make matters worse, we often further romanticize our past. Not that our history needs further embellishment or romance. How can you romanticize the drama of one of the greatest battles of Islam, the battle of *Mu'ta* (629), near Karak, where Arab armies, led by tight-belted, flowing-robes and bandy-legged leaders, inexperienced in the art of organized warfare, proved themselves proudly against the mighty Byzantine legions? Let flash through your mind at that fateful battle Jaffar al-Tayyar a direct cousin of the Prophet, fierce and yet full to the brim with his gentle faith, or King Aminadab, the Nabateans of Petra, King Herod, Shurahbil ben Hasnah, Umayyad caliphs who built desert spas and castles, al-Humaymah, from whence the Abbasside Caliphate originated, the Roman legionnaires and their Caesars, Salah al-Din and his crusader adversary, Richard the Lion-hearted. Such names, such history ... passionate, arduous, merciful, and bloody. The night and day in one filament, burning to light human history for all time. A glorious caravan of historical personalities and ideas, each leaving a mark, a landmark along the King's highway of human existence.

Too much history in the land. Both old and new, this land has made legends. In this century alone, this land has created a few legends, something to match the legends of old and significant enough to be recorded. The Great Arab Revolt with the gentle looking yet fierce-hearted, Sharif Hussein of Mecca, son of the proudest house of all Arabia, and the noblest and oldest family in the world. His dreamy-eyed son, King Faisal, a desert princeling who suddenly found himself in the web of intrigue in the corridors of the League of Nations, San Remo, London, and Paris. Odeh Abu Tayyih, the gentle and the fierce combined, Sheikh of the Hwaitat tribe, a Bedouin nationalist of deep loyalties. Remember, it was in Amman that the last Islamic Caliphate was declared. Abdullah, son of Hussein, the bridge of centuries, wise and far ahead of his time and experienced in the art of modern and traditional diplomacy. It is here and now that even an obscure British captain became a legend … Lawrence of Arabia; even the name has a ring. Not to mention Glubb Pasha and many, many others. Hussein, the quiet charisma, of whom I shall speak later.

Only God knows how much history is in the land. There were prophets by the dozen, some recorded and others only in the hearts of the people. The oral tradition continues its march and keeps the flame lit. We bide our time; we hope to learn as we have learned in the past. For, this land, this Middle East, is used to change, peaceful and violent, small, and big, ideological, spiritual, and physical, and it has endured as it shall. There is too much investment to quit now. The challenge is seemingly very big, even overwhelming, but I, for one, do not despair. This decadence from which we suffer shall pass, for there is so much resilience left in our people that a leader shall emerge to bring back to life the phoenix to our lives. The ashes of the 20th century will once more cleanse our souls, and something new will emerge.

If I sound like a prophet, it is because this is in the tradition of my people, and in the sands of my land I, too, have drunk from the Holy River, and am made from its mud and clay, as are my people. We talk because we like to communicate, and we find medicine in the word. It is loaded with the aphrodisiac of our history and poetry, and it helps us gloss over what we cannot have, and what is rightfully ours. It eases the pain of the present helplessness by keeping alive our humanity. Shall we, are we are asked to, surrender so completely that we cannot even communicate to ourselves our history, our dreams, our reality? Again, if I talk and sound like a nationalist humanist, it is because I am, with no apologies offered. This, too, shall pass, and this land, the Jordan Valley kissing both banks and touching the hills of Palestine and Jordan, the cradle of civilization now so utterly degraded it cannot defend itself, the land of the prophets and heroes, shall once more produce a savior.

Jesus lived in Palestine and died there, but his holy feet touched the lands called Jordan. Shall we forget that? Mohammad Ibn Abdullah PBUH, the Prophet of Islam, in the only miracle associated with him, that of *Isra'*, his nocturnal journey from Holy Mecca to Holy Jerusalem, blessed Jerusalem, and the lands around it. So many of the prophet Mohammad's *Sahabeh*, companions and friends and leaders, came from Jordan or lived in it that it is hard to count them all. Shall that be forgotten too?

That is what we are asked to do, and that is the heart breaker. Lie down and slumber in our new helplessness and inefficiency. We try that once in a while. I have tried to forget, as I will try, yet a memento here, a *Maqam*, landmark, there, a poem, a religious ceremony I listen to on the radio, a passing remark by a friend, my daughtes' questions arouse in me an intensity of feeling and emotion. An emotion for which I cannot and do not wish to apologize. Often, we are accused of being emotional, as if emotions were a shameful curse. Often, we get so shocked by the "accusation" that we do not know what to say. I wonder what is wrong with emotions. I think that is what separates us from beasts of prey, and that is why we were made in God's image. What is man without sentiment or emotion? An automaton? A depersonalized, homogenized extension of the machine? A beast? I often wonder, also, whether Hitler had any emotions at all; and what about all the beasts like Hitler? Surely, they take the shape of man and are in His image, but just as surely, they have nothing to do with humanity.

The Palestinians and the Jordanians: Shifting Numbers

My soul, my people's soul is bare in this century. The flesh has been stripped from it and a parade of Orientalists, scientists, politicians, statesmen and scholars is studying us. Not only the land, but our souls are being raped and raped again. We, the Jordanians and Palestinians, an extension of our Arab tribe, look for a touch of understanding and sympathy in a world where the art of cruelty has reached a very high level. We suffer from our emotions, our humanity, and we feel trapped in a never-ending corridor of intrigue, cruelty, and hatred. The Jordan is only a river, a geographic expression that is supposed to join two lands; yet in this century, it has succeeded in separating two peoples. I like to think of the Palestinians as West Jordanians, but they like to think of themselves as Palestinians. After all, is not nationalism, to a large degree, only a feeling? They and we are experts in the art of suffering, for it is not only the ailing who feels the pain. Those around him often suffer more, and though the ailing, in his ailment, may not know it, the suffering of those around is just as real, and often more so.

In this century, we have mixed like we never mixed before. For, *Jund al-Urdun*, the Jordan district and *Jund Falastin*, the Palestine district, had always mixed before, their boundaries changing with the changing of times and rulers, often divided from east to west, latitudinally, but at times along the present division lines of north/south, longitudinally. For over a 1,000 years now, Palestine and Jordan have been known along almost the present boundaries. Now a giant mixing machine called the West has thrown us together. And here we are loving and hating it, constantly adjusting, and readjusting to the new "realities", the new "facts of life". Who are the Jordanians? The

Palestinians? Where are they? Can we not find a new expression like Pale-Jordanians? Jorpalians? Jorstinians? I wonder if we should, if we could, for the proud Palestinians, though so ethnically, religiously, geographically, and linguistically similar, enjoy or suffer distinct traditions and experiences. Why should they become anything but Palestinians, in the same sense that one wonders why should two brothers be alike?

In the eyes of the world, or so have Hollywood and western propaganda portrayed, all Jordanians are Bedouins, nomads. Not that there is any objection to this in itself, for, in fact, it is a mark of distinction for many Jordanians to claim Bedouin descent. The objection is to the implications and shadows such statements hold. For, the Bedouins are supposedly not attached to a particular plot of land; they are *ruhhal*, or "roamers" of the desert, they do not belong anyplace! They are difficult to identify and to count.[1] Many Jordanians are Bedouins, or of Bedouin stock. Right now, it is estimated that of the almost 2.2 million people of Jordan's east bank, about 5% are Bedouins. But there are other Jordanians who live in villages, and till the arid land and make it produce, and there is where the majority of people lived until about a decade ago. Now most Jordanians live in the capital, Amman, and surrounding areas or in larger towns like Zarka, Irbid, Salt or Karak. Yet, the idea that Jordanians are nothing but a handful

---

1. The 1979 Census calculates the numbers of Bedouins as 10,000. They were about 59,000 according to the 1961 Census.

of Bedouins is still maintained, no doubt an attempt to create an image that there are no people on the land, or that Jordan is a land without a people.

This makes Jordanians doubly bitter: once because they are there and they are ignored. Their numbers are being inflated or deflated, according to the whim of whoever does the counting. Their bitterness increases because they have no way of countering such absurd juggling of statistics, and also because of their fear, lest they hurt the feelings of Palestinian brethren, since a certain sensitivity has developed over this issue. Secondly, because there is a blatant attempt at recreating the false impression that once was given to Palestine … a land without a people, a false image that helped pave the way for the creation of the state of Israel. The world was provided the image that the Jewish settlers were not imposing on anybody, that they were going to an empty land, a desert, to make it bloom!

Now there is an attempt to create the image that Jordan, too, is or was a land without a people, that whatever Jordanians exist are nomadic Bedouins who do not really count. This attempt is made in a very clever way, designed to confuse and to obfuscate the statistics. Often, Jordanians are referred to only as a handful of Bedouin supporters of the regime. Statistics "accidentally" and often intentionally slip into the statements of certain Western leaders or Zionist writers, that what we have in Jordan is King Hussein and "his supporters" – the Bedouin army. The "estimates" of Palestinians reach high, with most "analysts" or statement-makers settling around the figure of 60% of Jordan's population being Palestinian. This is embarrassing to the Jordanians for several reasons. For one, they have no way to counter this at local, regional, or international information levels. For another, even if they do resent the political implications, they feel embarrassed denying them, for then they would appear "provincial" and narrow-minded. Unfortunately, even some Arab leaders, knowingly or unknowingly, repeat these figures. Reasons for this juggling of the figures are many, but the most obvious and certainly the most dangerous is that the Palestinians can and should settle in this empty land, and forget Palestine.

The contradiction of this attempt is not hard to pinpoint by the reasonable reader or careful analyst, for whom it is not designed. It is designed for the average citizen in Europe or America, who has neither the time nor, perhaps, the inclination to research the facts. The romantic Lawrence of Arabia saga of a Bedouin Jordan is maintained, but now not all for romantic reasons. For, if Palestine had been empty, to begin with, when the Jewish immigrant waves arrived, why are there Palestinian refugees in Jordan and elsewhere, and why is there a need to find them a home? But who has the time, the patience, or the tools to research the truth at all times? Especially in this day and age, when "information" and "propaganda" techniques have reached high levels of sophistication? Often an obscure statement planted in the right place, or an innuendo in another, leave a more lasting image then scholarly works do. The arm of modern-day propaganda techniques reaches the heart and soul of people everywhere. Pseudo-intellectual magazines like Time and Newsweek are read by people the world over. Often the tidbit of "truth" is planted in the most unlikely places ... in a book, a television program or a film that has nothing to do with the Arab world.

It is frustrating because it is a denial of reality and a super-imposition of other images over it. Jordan, like Palestine, was never a land without a people. Ottoman records from the 16th century on speak of the East Bank as a densely populated area. The records are available and speak for themselves. According to the British records, Jordan's population in 1940 was 440,000, not including the Bedouins. At that time, Jordan's Bedouin population must have exceeded 150,000, which brings Jordan's population then and now to about one half that of the Palestinian population. Which means that there are now well over one million Jordanians living in Jordan, the East Bank. Jordan's inhabitants are currently about 2.2 million people. The argument is really a moot one, for, even if they had been a minority, does this mean the Palestinians should settle in Jordan and give up their rights in Palestine? Certainly not. But the attempt at creating this impression continues. Nor, do I think, it is possible or acceptable for the Palestinian people, who suffered displacement, mistreatment, and the denial of national dignity, to agree to an unjust act committed against them. The fact remains that it really does not matter whether or not they are a minority in Jordan. This has nothing to do with their rights in Palestine, nor with the fact that they are very welcome in Jordan, and are indeed in their home. If they wish to stay, so be it.

The Palestinians

The Palestinians are a very dynamic people who have played a major role in the modern history of Jordan, contributing substantially to the country's development in all fields. Their self-consciousness helped to generate a Jordanian self-consciousness that hitherto had found little impetus or motive for development. The Palestinians, a people deprived of land, legitimacy, self-expression, self-rule or indeed a national identity, became a terrific motivating force in Jordan. Consciously or otherwise, the Jordanians began to emulate their Palestinian brethren, first in outward appearance and mannerisms, and later in the more fundamental ways of life, like the Palestinian emphasis on education and self-reliance.

The Palestinians, long subjected to the indignity of British direct rule, and having helplessly witnessed their country opened to one wave of Jewish immigrants after another, developed a sense of consciousness much earlier. British heavy-handedness, and more often total disregard for the most basic human rights of Palestinians, taught them some very bitter lessons. The forced Jewish immigration and settlement into Palestine added further frustration. It is here that the Palestinians learned to mistrust authority and to develop a certain negative attitude towards it. They were forced, almost literally, to lie still while their land was opened up to Russians, Poles and Germans whose religion happened to be Jewish. They learned to be in opposition, for they never assumed, nor were they permitted to assume, any responsibility. Their lives were touched, drastically changed, and manipulated against their will. The final blow came with the decision of the British to withdraw from Palestine, an act unique in history, after having permitted the Jewish settlers to arm themselves, then assuring them of military victory, while leaving the Arab population defenseless, weaponless, and leaderless. The Palestinian population, predominantly rural, was forced out of home and land. Overnight they became a destitute lot of refugees at the mercy of international dole and relief. If they have learned anything, it is that they should value education over everything else. An educated man with skill is a free man. He can take his education with him. He cannot carry his house, his land, or his property.

Their arrival in Jordan expanded the horizons of this country, its population, and resources, both material and human. They brought with them a healthy respect for modernity, knowledge, and an awareness of the 20th century. The Jordanians response to the Palestinian plight was that of local sympathy, and empathy. The Jordanians opened and continue to open their minds and hearts to their brothers, the Palestinians, and it is here and nowhere else in the world that the Palestinians have been accepted as full partners and citizens. And it is also here where they proved themselves as an intelligent, hard-working, and hardy people. The two peoples with two different experiences and identities quickly became a socially cohesive group. They separate over certain political issues and experiences; otherwise, the two peoples are one. Most Jordanians and Palestinians lament the necessity of identifying themselves separately, though they realize the necessity for this at regional and international levels.

At first bewilderment, then shock, then frustration. The Palestinians expected to return, and they lived as most still do, with the hope that they would return home. But as the weeks turned into months, then years, and now three decades, bitter and deep frustration set in. The tents turned into tin shanties, mud cottages, and then brick and even some stone. The camps became a permanent fixture of Jordan's scene, adding another piece to its mosaic, a bitter and alienated piece. A square peg in a round hole. The Palestinians learned to live in an alienating environment. The children of the land of milk and honey, Palestine, a hard-working and ambitious people, were reduced to a status of poverty in a land that is not their own.

Their feelings of alienation and anger were compounded by the slowly dawning realization that their Arab brethren were unwilling or unable to help them liberate their land. They, and many others, including sometimes myself, could not understand or accept the seeming helplessness of the Arabs in facing the Zionist danger.

How is it that a nation of three million people, gathered from the four corners of the globe and speaking different languages, can defeat the Arab *Ummah*, the Arab Nation? Many could not, and still cannot, understand why or how; and if they do, they cannot accept it as a permanent state of affairs.

1948 and its aftermath: The tension and the price

Jordan's political and social life, serene in the 1920s, 1930s and well into the 40s was suddenly changed. Sir John Bagot Glubb, commander of the Arab Legion (1939-1956), describes Jordan in that period as one of the happiest and quietest places on earth. But then, Glubb was speaking for himself, a sentiment that was not shared by many others. Jordan's attempt at rehabilitating what was left of Palestine into its own entity soon commenced.

The Jordanian leaders, perhaps unaware of the depth, intensity, and resistance of the Palestinians, gauged their mood on different levels. King Abdullah I dared say what no other Arab leader would admit. As a realistic and experienced man, he admitted the then unthinkable. Other Arab leaders with their newly found independence, and lacking the knowledge and experience necessary for the task, spoke otherwise. In hindsight, it is possible that they, too, like the people, could not understand what was happening or how to deal with it. In fact, perhaps no Arab, then or now, understands what is really going on. For, truly, how does a state as small as Israel maintain such a hold on the imagination of the entire Western world, and also control it for so long? How can Israel, really, with its umbilical cord linked to the United States, dictate the policy of that nation with regard to the Middle East? Rationalizations may be found, but it remains bewildering and difficult to comprehend.

The frustration was compounded by successive defeats, big and small. Many coups d'état, many changes, violent and peaceful. Political ideologies and political parties began to emerge. Many leaders paid the price for their frustration with their lives. King Abdullah I was shot in one of the holiest mosques of Islam, al-Aqsa, in Jerusalem. The nation was shocked at the use and intensity of violence, for the Arabs, Jordanians, or Palestinians are a peaceful people and more prone to compromise than to rigidity.

Yet physical, verbal, and mental violence has never abated since then. Several levels of frustration and defeat are still stacked upon each other. With the creation of Israel, a veil of sadness has settled on Jordan, and indeed on the Middle East. Young and old, professional and layman, soldier and civilian, feel the intensity of the defeat that sears the soul, indeed, of the successive defeats with no end in sight. Year in and year out, no Moslem or Christian feast has been celebrated properly; the customary announcement comes via radio, TV, and the newspapers, that this year the celebrations will be confined to religious prayers only in mosques and churches. Again, we celebrate the infamous dates of November 2, November 22, May 15, June 5, October 6, and so on, dates of defeat and shame. Dates when we were attacked both bodily and mentally, and slowly but surely more lands were lost, more waves of refugees, more camps were made. Yet, still more hopes that the next time will be better. On several days of the week, our radio stations broadcast messages from Palestinians to their families, relatives and loved ones. I do not like to listen to these messages, for they break my heart and burn my soul. The Arab is a family man, a person who likes his group of people. Listen to one of them. The message sender is an ordinary person, speaks very quickly, even haltingly, as if embarrassed at what he or she is doing. Often, they stutter and trail off. It goes something like this. "*Assalamu alaikum*", peace be unto you. I am Ameeneh or Ali so and so, from Ramallah, and I wish to tell all those who love us, relatives, and friends, that we are in good health. I wish to say hello to my brother Ahmad and family in Kuwait to my brother Mustafa in Saudi Arabia, to my aunt Salmah and her family and children in Australia, if they can hear me, and to my sister in America. God bless you and please tell us how you are. We still do not know where cousin Sami is. Good-bye". A sad message from a sad people that keeps trying.

That is why it is difficult to speak about the Jordanians without speaking about the Palestinians, for both peoples are united now by so many bonds it is difficult, if not impossible, to untangle them.

I often wonder at how good we are at communicating with each other, and yet how difficult it is for us to communicate with others. Is it because we are basically a peaceful, compromising people who cannot cope with the violence of the

20th century and its internal changes and external challenges? Why is it that we have to pay the price of western cruelty to our cousins the Jews? In a recent issue of the Paris-based Arabic magazine *al-Mustaqbal*, the Future, I read an article on how the Germans have lost the guilt feeling they had because of their mistreatment of the Jews in World War II. The lead article in the magazine, with a cartoon of Hitler on the front cover, gave the impression that this was a positive development. I wonder if it is, though I do not wish the Germans any ill will. Did the Germans, the West, pay their just price? And is this price, by any standard, equal to what we have paid and will continue to pay for a long time? Was the indemnity equal to the deed, and who will pay our indemnity?

The price we are paying is that we are taught day in and day out how to become cruel and appreciate the value and the worth of violence and death machines. We continue to build an army composed of civilians, peasants and merchants who do not have the traditional hard-hearted professionalism of the western soldier. Many of our soldiers, and I say this with a certain sense of pride, are still farmers and civilians who happen to be wearing khaki clothes. Even after four successive wars, we have not taught our soldier how to become an artist at killing. Yet, I believe, slowly but surely we are learning, and I wish we were not! One day we shall definitely master the technique.

Looking back at our history, I find no Genghis Khan or a Hulagu. In only isolated instances, and usually under tremendous stress, has violence been committed unnecessarily. Our culture never had, and does not now have; a game of blood: no dog, bull or cock fighting. All the games we have are games of skill, not games of killing. The sword dance, or rather the dueling with the sword that we have is also more of a dance to show the skill of players and the gracefulness of their movements. The repugnance we hold for the spilling of blood at any time is a trait we are unaware of. Yet, how many times has the world witnessed Palestinian youth, trained to kill or to carry out a particular hijacking operation, giving themselves up at the last minute? When faced with the ultimate of killing innocents, the Arab youth, though having trained for months for that operation, simply could not do it. Local tradition and lore are replete with tales of two tribes or two villages that battled or raided each other. Sometimes hundreds on each side, yet the end result was always surprisingly very few killed or wounded ... "Mahmoud was shot in the leg ... two dead horses, one man dead." Surprising results ... at least I always thought so.

In this tradition, and in spite of the many violent attempts at his life, or to topple the regime, King Hussein has meticulously avoided violent retaliation. Men who conspired against his life have been forgiven, many released to hold important positions later on ... a few even becoming Cabinet ministers.

We are paying the price by being forced to devote so much time and energy to the struggle, time and energy that we should be devoting to the development of a better life for our people. The doctor, the engineer, the child, the factory laborer, the housewife, the teacher ... are constantly preoccupied with the dangerous challenge posed by Israel. It is so close, one can almost smell the gunpowder and hear the guns while observing Israeli warplanes roaming the skies of the Middle East, searching to "teach" somebody a lesson.

We sleep at night wondering, will tonight be it? Will we be attacked? Will war begin in the morning? We are always ready for bad news; we have grown accustomed to listening for it. Sometimes, I, we, wish there were some new elements, some changes. Yet, almost always, like a clock ticking our lives away, we listen to the same news, and when there is some change, it is usually not pleasant. An attack on the refugee camps in South Lebanon, the arrest of high school children in the West Bank, a new arms deal for Israel.

We have also learned to live with shaky Arab regimes, and there is no country in the area that is not constantly regarded as a candidate for the next coup d'état. The new faces come with the refurbished old slogans that we have been hearing for the last three decades. New alignments are made, adjustments here and there between the various regimes of the area, and very soon things settle down to the old routine, and new intrigues commence. In the meantime, visits are exchanged, "historical" decisions are taken, startling statements are uttered; old enemies meet on neutral ground, kiss each other and shake hands, and once again they discover they have always been friends and on the same side.

For most of my life, this comic drama has been repeated with such regularity that it has become, in a perverse way, almost comforting. The vast majority of our people has been born since the *Nakbeh*, the tragedy. The *Nakbeh* refers to the creation of the state of Israel in 1948. I feel sorry for our children having to grow up in an atmosphere of protracted and seemingly never-ending conflict. Is this how the people lived during the Hundred Years War? I wonder, for our war has lasted only 30 years if we start counting from 1948, or 60 years if we start from 1920.

Very few people have been harassed like we have, whether on the individual or the national level. We always feel cornered ... sometimes trapped. A Jordanian businessman, or a Palestinian professor or doctor holding a Jordanian passport, is passing through some European airport. There is a line behind him; the passport officer looks up, motions him to stand aside. He is thoroughly searched. His fellow passengers glance suspiciously at him. That is another price. We have become the bad boys of the world. Who gave us that image? It makes us feel like an intrusion on the civilized world. What have we done to become the anti-hero of humanity? Why can we not be understood? For, if we have any violence at all it is only verbal violence; it releases our tensions and acts like a catharsis to our souls.

The Kenyans, Colombians or Sri Lankans, and most other people in the developing world, have only their internal challenges to meet: How to develop their countries, raise their standard of living and achieve a better way of life. Everybody who is capable, East or West, is trying to help.

We, the Jordanians, Palestinians, Arabs, have this, plus having to cope with the daily violent threat to our existence. We had to pick one of the most formidable minority groups in the world for our adversary. Or did we pick them? A minority that, in one way or another, captured the imagination of the Western world in this century and seems to continue to hold on to it. We cannot admit defeat because of its totality and enormity, and at the same time, we cannot let go of the struggle. You see, Palestine, so close to Jordan that the dust and the people have become one, is the heart of the Arab world. If you look at the map of Palestine, now called Israel, you will see it is in the shape of a dagger in the heart of the area. Its present boundaries, among many other factors, sever the geographic land continuity of the Arab world. That is why I am always touched, as I am touched when listening to Sheikh Abdul Basit Mohammad Abdul Samad raising the call for the prayer on Radio Amman ... "*Allahu Akbar* ... God is greater ...*" it is a call to prayer in praise of the Lord, yet it also sounds like a lamentation. For when an Arab feels confused or lost or incapable of doing something, he exclaims "*Allahu Akbar*" to vent his frustration. The Sheikh speaks for me, for the Jordanians, and for all the Arabs. Once, Allal al-Fasi, the late Moroccan national leader, told me that since 1948, no joyous drum or song has been sung with heart in Morocco. That gives me more hope, for in the Sheikh's voice, sad, undulating, and beautiful, I also detect a determination, a resilience, a defiance.

The Jordanians and Palestinians are now one people, and no political loyalty, however strong, will separate them permanently; nor do I think either side would wish such a separation. It is difficult to stereotype both or either, in the same sense that it is difficult to stereotype a Frenchman or an Italian. Everyone speaks the Arabic language and only about 8% are Christians, with the rest Sunni Muslim. Small religious communities of Bahai and Druze exist, and a colorful variety of ethnic groups is also present. Among these are Circassians, Chechens, Armenians, Assyrians, Kurds and Turkmen. Some gypsies also live in Jordan. All form a harmonious pattern in the mosaic of Jordan's Middle Eastern society.

Dead Sea. Gorge, 1900–1920.
G. Eric and Edith Matson, American Colony (Jerusalem).
Photo Department. Library of Congress.
Restoration by Kelvin Bown. *Reawakening the Past*, 2017.

Chapter Two

Development and Change: Causes and Range

Enough has been written about the factors that eventually lead a society to change in response to changing circumstances or to real or imagined challenges it thinks it faces. For Jordan and the Arab world, there is no question that contact with the West, in the modern era, was of great importance. Yet, it cannot, and indeed it does not, explain the whole story. When the image of a people about themselves, their place in the world and their destiny is shaken so severely, as happened in the case of Arab society, the impact is momentous. Arab society's contact with the West since the early 19th century has not been a gentle affair of cultural, economic, or diplomatic exchange. Rather, it has been the association of a technologically and militarily superior adversary with a less advanced society. For the Arab society and the Arab individual, Western superiority was shocking. It was all the more shocking since Arab Muslim society, centuries after the glorious day of Islam, still cherished the image of its own superiority.

At state level, and in every state in the Arab world, an active search was set in motion to ascertain the factors underlying Western superiority. From Mohammad PBUH to the present-day Arab leaders, the first need was always to acquire the military skills that would enable them to defend themselves against this intrusion. The Officers-Leaders soon realized that self-defense could not be achieved solely by acquiring military skills, and that they should espouse social reform as well as socialist and nationalistic ideologies; that the change needed must be comprehensive, covering every walk of life, and that reforming the military was not enough to check Western inroads and intrusions.

At individual level, the process was initially that of imitation of Western manners, dress styles and tastes. Later, however, the process of becoming *franji*-like became a genuine end in itself. "Westernization" became native since it demonstrated its worth and its practicality even at the level of the individual. Kemal Ataturk, founder of modern Turkey, spoke for individuals and nations alike when he stated that "before the impetuous torrent of civilization resistance is futile: it is quite without mercy towards the heedless and the refractory. In the face of the might and superiority of civilization, which pierces mountains, flies in the sky, sees everything from the atoms invisible to the eye of the stars, and which enlightens and investigates, nations striving to advance with a medieval mentality and primitive superstitions are condemned to perish or at least be enslaved and humiliated..." It would seem

Ataturk, as is the case with every leader in the developing countries today, was not speaking only of military prowess. The realization that total change is a necessity is implicit in every utterance made by these leaders today.

Jordan: External Factors

Had one taken a snapshot of Jordan in the early 1940s, one might have found a quiet, rather contented little country on the sidelines of regional and world affairs. The Palestine Problem, later called the Middle or Near East Problem and then the Arab-Israeli conflict, and now once more the Palestine Problem, helped change the situation. Jordan was thrust into a vortex of events whose dimensions and depth continue to be well beyond its power and means to handle. Leaving aside the external difficulties created and imposed by the Palestine Problem on Jordan and other Arab countries, with all its ugliness, enormity, and complexity, that problem has had both a positive and a negative effect on Jordan's life and society, in every sphere of activity, whether social, economic, or political. Negative, in that it thrust hundreds of thousands of destitute, confused, and directionless refugees into an already overstrained economy in a very short span of time. The dislocations were so enormous, it is a wonder that Jordan was ever able to deal with them at all. Positive, in that it introduced into Jordan's society a vast array of human resources whose energies and potential have played an important role in its development. Men have always differed on the definition of happiness, or its antithesis. They agree even less on that stage in between, limbo. At least politically, Jordan, whose existence is real yet whose being is in question, has remained in that state since 1948.

Development is best defined as the better control, direction and manipulation by man of his environment for his own good. Is this an economic, social or political definition? I do not know. But with all its seeming simplicity, this definition offers a deep insight into the issue of development and the race between the real and the potential, between the forces of change and those of tradition, between time and aspirations. Thus, development becomes a continuing process whose major characteristic is the expansion of the means of society to deal with problems. Countries blessed with stability, or whose existence is not in question, have only to grapple with their internal economic and political resources. Countries not so blessed, like Jordan, and with a menacing neighbor that frequently unleashes its forces of aggression, have to deal with a double challenge: internal and external. They are kept constantly on the run, yet are asked to deal with what has euphemistically been called the "Revolution of Rising Expectations". How does Jordan fare? What are the effects of development on its society?

Perhaps the most important aspect of the development of Jordan, from the early 1940s to the present, is its jump from a semi-primitive to a consumer and services society, without passing through the various agonizing stages of the industrial or even agricultural revolutions.[2] But then, that is not unique to Jordan. Political realities in many countries have necessitated such a jump, regardless of the price. The term primitive society, as used here, is not pejorative. A primitive or semi-primitive society largely produces what it consumes and its expectations of life do not usually extend beyond its means.

Only a generation ago, almost four-fifths of Jordan's population lived either a pastoral existence or in villages and in small towns. The change one observes today is not only in terms of urban versus rural residence, but in physical as well as psychological terms. Not only have the dress styles changed to become "Westernized" and "modern", change also occurred in consumer habits, in food consumption and calorie intake, and also in psychological and attitudinal terms. The traditional garb is giving way to modern dress and, whereas previously a man or a woman would own two or three *Thobs*, long garments, that too has changed in most cases, reflecting different Western styles. With the move from the rural or desert areas to urban life, a whole lifestyle that existed for millennia is changing and a new rhythm is replacing the old, relaxed, one. The goat-hair tent, the camel and individual independence of the desert Bedouins are virtually gone, perhaps forever. The rural areas are changing their aspect as well. Gone is the earthen-ware *Taboon*, oven, and bread is bought from modern bakeries. Also

---

2. See Appendix I contrasting certain socio-economic indicators for 1952 and 1975

gone is the *Mooneh*, household provisions that the family used to stock for the entire year and which used to consist of *Jamid*, dry yogurt, olives, olive oil, pickles, home-made cheese, tomato paste, jams, *burghul*, cracked wheat and other basic provisions. The average family was so well stocked that for most of the year all they needed to purchase were fresh fruits, vegetables, or meat.

Working in an office or a factory does not teach punctuality alone, but, in due process, a healthy respect for time and a certain amount of emphasis on efficiency in the performance of one's duties. The competition one faces in an urban environment necessitates such changes. And although a new arrival to the city carries with him a certain amount of loyalty to his family, kin and tribe, his very move, by definition, has moved him one step or more away from his group. This process of loosening ties with the extended kin, family or tribal group, brought about by the necessity of acquiring a new job or skill through one's personal efforts and initiative leads in time to a new emphasis on one's own interest, perhaps a little more sophistication and materialism and eventually, perhaps, to a questioning of one's loyalty to his kin group. The labor union, the professional association, the club no doubt begin to replace the old loyalties. This process is not unique to Jordan, where it is now taking place. Old habits and loyalties die hard, and in stages. Today's average Jordanian is in a state of transition between the old and the new ways of life; the process is still in progress.

The Role of Government

The government's role in effecting change is seen in almost every aspect of life. Economically, in the early 1960s, the government instituted the process of socio-economic planning. Since then, it has initiated the Five-Year Plan (1962–1967), later replaced by the Seven-Year Plan (1964–1970), the Three-Year Plan (1972–1975), and the Five-Year Plan (1976–1980). The government encourages private enterprise and initiates economic projects that the private sector is unwilling or unable to undertake. It is currently a major partner in the 30 largest economic and industrial companies in Jordan.

Socially, the government has been very active in the field of health, education, and welfare. Not the least of its efforts is its emphasis on the value and honor of manual labor and, more recently, on attempting to take a leading role in promoting changes in the role and status of women. Certainly, the government's efforts at asserting its authority in settling disputes between individuals and groups were a prime factor behind the abolishing of the Tribal Law in 1975. By a variety of methods, insurance companies in Jordan have come to replace the custom of the *diyyah* (blood money) paid by the family of the accused to the family of a deceased or injured party as the result of a crime, whether accidental or intentional. Though it cannot be substantiated, the government has accepted and, no doubt, has come to welcome this practice. The government encourages individuals and groups to settle disputes through the formal processes of the courts. As a result, one observes in today's Jordan more formality and legalism in the handling of affairs between individuals and groups.

A generation ago, the state in Jordan, like its sisters in many other developing countries in the world, was no more than a "policeman", regulating the flow of citizen's affairs, with little interference except where and when absolutely necessary. Today's Jordan is a welfare state where the affairs of people are regulated and manipulated in the fields of health, education, welfare, economy and even in attitudes and opinions.

As a result, one witnesses in today's Jordan the rise of new classes and new leaders that replace the old classes and the old elite. A middle class with bourgeois tastes and attitudes is definitely a reality, with emphasis on material acquisition and a "keeping up with the Joneses" attitude. Military officers, bureaucrats, groups of intelligentsias, professional groups, clubs and a genuine labor movement with some class consciousness have also developed.

The change, tilted, uneven and incomplete, is still in progress. Its directions and final outcome are not yet clear, and cannot be clearly delineated as yet.

External factors including the Western intrusions and its Zionist manifestation, Israel, into Arab society, politically, militarily, economically, and culturally, have necessitated living beyond one's means, often on borrowed money. There has been a terrific need and pressure to modernize very quickly. Surely, both masses and leaders of the Arab countries were aware of the challenges facing them and the price to be paid. The shock of this intrusion made the price seem appropriate.

Indigenous Factors

But that is not the whole story. Arab society, including that of Jordan, did not change solely in response to outside challenges. Forces from within were always present, often dormant in previous centuries, but never absent. The glorious Quran eloquently stated that "God does not change a people unless they change within themselves." A *Hadith*, a saying of the Prophet, states: "Raise your children for an age that is not yours," while it is one of the *Sharia*, religious laws, axioms, to adhere to the principle that "judgments change with the changing times". The clear implication is that change is a positive force, that the will and awareness to change is inherent in the nature of a society, and that change is not exclusively a response to external factors. Thus, change would have come to Arab and Jordanian society even if there had not been external challenges, albeit at a less accelerated rate.

The shrinkage of the world in the 20th century in response to the impact of improvements in communication and transportation facilitated not only the movement of objects and people, but of ideas as well. Good ideas never lack an audience. They are like a weed that craves light and thrives on crossbreeding, often growing better when stepped on.

Development and change are ideas that have captured the imagination of humanity everywhere. It is an anomaly that change often takes the shape of a haphazard metamorphosis rather than a deliberate process of transformation. Happily, change in Jordan has taken the latter: that of deliberate and planned process, though the planning is not always complete.

Historically, change in the Western experience came as a result of uncontrolled forces unleashed before and after the breakdown of the feudal system. This breakdown was coupled with the introduction of new modes of production, the rise of modern cities and the emergence of new social classes and ideologies. The indigenous, evolutionary interaction of all these groups, ideas and forces had genuine grassroots support among the people, often in spite of the desires and wishes of the ruling elite. In the developing countries, most of the development and change was initiated by the positive will of the policymaker. While the idea of change is inherent in Arab society, it has had to be induced to catch up with the 20th century. This process of catching up, now many generations old, is far from complete.

As a subculture within Arab society, Jordan has had its share of suffering in the 20th century. Proud of its history and culture, it, too, was shocked with the reality of its inadequacies in the modern age, in addition to the challenges of the Palestine Problem. Its response was characteristic of certain human behavior under a stress situation, outwardly denying its shortcomings and manifesting a belligerent, though inadequate, stance, while inwardly imposing upon itself a severe process of evaluation and re-evaluation. As part of the predominant "culture of shame", this process was a necessity to "save face" in response to adverse challenges. Nothing else could, or should, have been expected. For, at the same time that the Arab accepts, and even secretly welcomes change, he has to pretend and proclaim that it has always been part of his culture and heritage. From the extreme left to the extreme right, Arab ideologies find justification in Arab history and culture. Yet, there remains within the Arab self the awareness that something is amiss, and needs to be corrected.

Jordan is no longer a static society. The processes of modernization, urbanization, industrialization, and development have left their heavy mark. The skyline of Jordan, as is the case with every Arab country, is studded with minarets and factory chimneys. The shape of the landscape itself has changed in response to the conscious desire for development. It is true that the social and economic change now taking place in Jordan covers the whole spectrum of life. But it is equally true that the change is still incomplete, and that its benefits are unevenly distributed. It may take a generation or more before equity makes itself present among the rising classes: the middle class, the intelligentsia, the bureaucracy, the army officers and the urban labor class. The old elite, landed and otherwise, has declined and is being replaced by new classes of people whose bases of power are modern and who are still struggling to maintain their newly acquired status. Within Jordan's urban centers, one can still witness the socio-economic disparity between various neighborhoods and sectors. The contrast is more glaring when one considers the gap between the urban, village and Badia[3] life. The disparities and the class distinctions are a fact of life, but a fully developed class consciousness has not, as yet, developed. It may take a long time before it can leave a mark in the economic or the political fields. The value of time has become a reality, at least in the urban centers. Women, in various stages of emancipation, are to be seen everywhere. Physical labor has increased not only in value but in prestige as well, and education has been given primacy heretofore unknown in Arab history.

Perhaps the most fundamental change is that the idea of change itself has been consciously accepted, even welcomed as a fact of life. What is traditional, unless it is fundamental and exceedingly basic, is no longer simply sacrosanct and unquestioned. The idea of development and positive change is no longer feared, except by small pockets of resistance here and there. The breakdown of the tribal and the extended patriarchal family relationships and authority are welcomed by the majority of the people. Multiple marriages, though in certain circumstances permitted in principle by religious authority and sanction, are no longer unquestionably, completely socially desirable. Life has acquired a new tempo of modernity, whose dimensions extend beyond the realm of words and theory into reality.

Jordan, a Moslem country, has always accepted two basic tenets of Islamic society and tradition. The first is a most fundamental

3. Badia means desert area

tenet dealing with social mobility as an accepted and welcomed fact. Since all people are equal in the sight of God, who bestows His blessings on whomever He chooses, there are no social distinctions and no rigidly inherited status. Thus, achievement in Moslem society has always been merit-oriented. This idea received further impetus in the 20th century. The second is that change is a basic fact of life, whose dimensions are bound only by God's will and man's ability within that will.

Never completely isolated in previous eras, Jordan's Islamic society does not willfully wish to isolate itself in the 20th century either. Western travelers, writers, and film-makers, for reasons of their own, may have romanticized and made it appear an isolated Bedouin land. Yet, underneath this exotic and romantic image of Jordan, there lies a reality of response to the challenges and changes needed in real life. And while its leaders may have cultivated this romantic image, they induced and encouraged the necessary changes. To live in accordance with the terms of the 20th century, socio-economic development was a necessity. Otherwise, and as Ataturk succinctly stated, there was humiliation and possible enslavement. The awareness of such a danger has prompted the Arabs to change, Jordanians included. The Arabic proverb that "those who do not bow to the storm will be driven or be broken by it" has been a basic tenet of Arab life in this century.

In dealing with the process of development, Jordan has had the edge over its Arab neighbors. At the economic level, its policy has been characterized by the prudent use of its resources, both local and off-shore. Outside aid has been carefully utilized avoiding "white elephant" and extravagant projects. It has also been characterized by the humane treatment of local political opponents and their eventual integration and full utilization of their energies in Jordan's private and public life. No undue violence has ever been used in the treatment and rehabilitation of political adversaries into enthusiastic supporters. Local yeast that otherwise could have turned into a deadly virus was tamed and oriented towards more constructive endeavors. Protestors and adversaries were very wisely turned into ardent supporters and allies, and the "firebrands" were swiftly turned into "constructive elements". The realization set in early that a society that rids itself of all its opponents will quickly back-slide; surely, one may be eliminating the most creative. It is better to channel their energy and exploit it for the positive welfare of the society, if at all possible. Some may claim that the goal of such a society is not to do good, but simply to exist and to refrain from doing evil. Perhaps so. But then, is not the absence of evil, in itself, good? Yet Jordan has not simply refrained from violence; positive policies designed and directed towards the betterment of social and economic welfare of the people have also been pursued.

The state, any state, deals with power; it recognizes no other language. To do so, it must exist and assert itself in a variety of ways. From the 1920s to the 1940s, Jordan was a state whose existence went relatively unchallenged, both from within and from without. Since then, it has continuously faced many challenges. In assessing its response, one is struck by the tenacity with which it has maintained itself against very difficult odds, both political and economic. Adversity seems to have given Jordan endless new leases on life. Perhaps that is because it has been blessed by several factors of extreme importance. One is a conscious population aware of the internal and external challenges of modern times, and which has become very responsive to the call of the "revolution of rising expectations". Second, because of the existence of an intelligently active and aware leadership whose moderate methods and style have demonstrated both agility and initiative. Blessed with longevity and concern for the welfare of the people, this leadership has given social and economic content to the political ideas and slogans in vogue in the Arab world since the end of World War II. If anything character- izes the Jordanian experiment, or experience, it is a tenacious moderation whose dividends are clearly visible now in the economic and social fields. Not many explanations can be proffered for the continuing success of Jordan in the midst of so much intransigence and adversity, both from within and from without.

How can one measure the effects of development upon any society? Surely, it is easier to deal with numbers and quantities, but then, that is to partially avoid the crux of the matter. The unaware must surely be happy with their circumstances, for nothing exists but the reality of their situation. That, however, is not the case with Jordan since the 20th century thrust itself into its midst politically, militarily, economically, and socially. Both quantitatively and qualitatively, it has changed drastically, and it is perhaps too soon or too unfair to assess it now. But should the standards be those of the Western 20th century? The answer, no doubt, would be in the affirmative. The process of economic and social change has certainly made Jordan a changing society. The lifestyle has changed drastically in form and content. Even the physical shape of the landscape and the dress itself have changed. That is not a philosopher's illusion, nor the dream of a wild-eyed planner. That is a fact of life, consciously, or perhaps even subconsciously, desired by the people and their leaders. Calculated, in most cases, that development has had a terrific impact upon the lives of the people. The change, the development, is not yet complete. The process is still going on and its directions, while plausibly discernable, are not completely identified. Yet this development witnessed in Jordan, as indeed elsewhere in the Arab and the Third World, is a reality whose psychological and physical impact and influence is immeasurable. Jordan has succeeded in instilling in its people a new sense of national loyalty which required no mean effort on the part of its people and its leaders; a sense of nationhood that still needs further development should the political circumstances in the area permit.

Change: Considerations

We may look as though we were living in a state of moral schizophrenia, and for many individuals that, indeed, is the case, yet, our cultural heritage has such a hold that we find so many rationalizations that are morally satisfactory to ourselves, and thus we see no contradiction. Or was Lawrence right when he stated that "the Semite", and we are Semites, "can see black and white, a position and its antithesis, and accept both at the same time"? But to be a Jordanian, an Arab, now, you have to live not in one world, but in two worlds at the same time. In a way, and because of the transitory nature of change, its speed and intensity, it is like living in a no-man's land. Should you rely on your heritage and inherited values, mores, and tools, or should you partake of the present innovations coming from the industrialized world? Should you take from and rely on the time dimension, from the past? Or should you rely on the space dimension, taking from the present? The answer is not always easy and the self of a man is torn between the familiar and the new.

My father had few such dilemmas; my grandfather had none, for, both drank from one well of knowledge, and had only one source. For me and my generation, with our sources and resources, choices are limitless. The familiar attracts me, but innovation attracts me more. Often, we go on a shopping spree of values, ideas, and tools. Ours has become an eclectic approach, whereby we try to reconcile the old with the new. It is not easy to change old values and habits to new ones, and when we do, we invariably rationalize as we must. How else can we live with ourselves? We try to reconcile, but it is difficult. Some of us call it *al-Salah Wa al-Mu'asarah*, contemporaneousness and "vintageness". That is an attempt to select the vintage and the modern and maintain them side by side. That is what is happening right now, and we are at that stage where we end up with what I like to call a "hybrid", or a mutation; a wedding or a medley of the old and the new. In the conceptual and moral realm, it is another dimension of our societal mosaic where the pieces coexist side by side without blending, while the totality gives a complete whole and often an attractive effect.

Ideas are tyrannical, and once accepted by the conscious and the subconscious of a people, they are not easy to dislodge. In a way, most men become slaves to the myths they create or choose to believe in. That is why change is easier to observe on the surface, and difficult to fathom. That is why the old persists and has a strength all its own; a strength that sustains and keeps it, in a reduced place, perhaps, but a place nonetheless.

Three Jordanian images come to mind to illustrate these points. One flash of the mind is of three generations of Jordanian females walking together in downtown Amman. The grandmother with her traditional clothing, sure of her ways, her sources of knowledge and condescending towards new ideas and tools. She is only 60, yet she is sure of herself. Her daughter, only 40 is in contrast. She has shed the traditional clothing and wears a modern dress with long sleeves, and her head is "properly" covered up. She is not as sure of herself as her mother, and she wavers between what was and the possibilities around and ahead. The grand-daughter is wearing a short dress or a miniskirt. She goes to the university, has read many new books, listens to all types of music and is an avid moviegoer and fan of western music. She, too, is sure of her sources of knowledge, though they differ drastically from her grandmother's. She, too, is condescending towards her mother, torn between tradition and modernity, and is only mildly tolerant of her grandmother's old-fashioned ways. And the debate between them continues.

The second snapshot is not generational, it is spatial. Between the Central Bank of Jordan building and the livestock market, the distance is three or four kilometers, yet their tools and methodologies are from different ages. At the bank, modern accounting techniques and computers are used, whereas at the livestock market barter is still common.

The third flash is in time dimension, with a 45 or 50-year-old man who has seen so much change his real age is often closer to 400. He can remember Amman in the 1940s, a neglected, quiet, and sleepy village, and he sees it now as a thriving, seemingly ever-expanding metropolis. His mind is torn between the past and the possibilities ahead.

With the changing jobs, of ways of making a living, even the landscape itself changed, and with all these, the structure of the family, tribe and kith and kin group. Inwardly and outwardly the change is ever-present, and continuous. Now that the majority of the people live in urban areas, or what resemble urban areas, the old relationships within the family and the tribe had to change. The tribe and the *hamulah*, the extended family, is a nostalgic relic of the past. People refer to them only for identification, or to boast. Instead, and by economic necessity and pressure, the family now is a cellular affair of husband, wife, and children. Even the immediate older generation by and large has moved out: very few families are more than cellular.

The pressure of urban home economy has had other effects on the structure of the family and society. Polygamy now is not only difficult, it is improbable and perhaps even impossible. Economic pressure and the exhortations of moralists and educationalists, along with social pressure, have rendered the practice a relic of the past. I know of no case of any man, nor have I heard of such in the last few years, who has three or four wives. None. I have no friend, or friend of a friend, who has two. People divorce and marry again, but it is exceedingly rare to find anyone with more than one wife.

Urbanization, education and government effort have expanded educational possibilities and job horizons for women, whose place and status in the family and society are changing very rapidly. It is so very rare to see a veiled woman in Jordan that it is almost a tourist attraction, even for Jordanians. No longer secluded, now educated and often skilled, women are seeking and finding employment in factories, government offices, different professions and even in the police force. No one is talking anymore about women's emancipation. That seems to be a settled issue; the quest is how to open ranks for her for a more meaningful participation in public life. Women (since 1974) can be nominated and elected to Parliament. Three women are members of the National Consultative Council, an appointed body taking the place of Parliament, since that body cannot be elected due to the 1967 occupation of the West Bank by Israel. In the latest Cabinet, a woman was appointed minister of social development, and there is a woman on the Amman City Council.

'Amman, the town among the ruins of ancient Philadelphia.
Date unknown.
G. Eric and Edith Matson, American Colony (Jerusalem). Photo
Department. Library of Congress.
Restoration by Kelvin Bown. *Reawakening the Past*, 2012.

Chapter Three

Making a Living

Until about two decades ago, the majority of Jordan's inhabitants lived on farms and in rural areas. Education, the lure of the city and its amenities, and lack of adequate services in rural areas caused this situation to change. At best, dry farming was only a hazardous business, with the farmer and his family living under the constant terror of possible lack of rain. This, in addition to a variety of other negative factors, not the least of which was the lack of scientific and business-like farming, soil erosion and insufficient soil humus. So much has changed that by 1975 only 18% of the labor force worked in agriculture, while 19% worked in mining, manufacturing, electricity and construction, and the majority, 63% worked in the services sector. The Gross National Product in 1978 was JD708.2 million and per capita income was JD319.2. The share of agriculture in the national economy was 8.4% only, while the share of the public administration sector, manufacturing and mining, trade, defense services and transportation was 20.7%, 18.7%, 15.5%, 11.3% and 10.3% respectively. Almost 36% of working people were self-employed.

Jordan's labor market had about 382,600 workers in 1975, which amounted to about 19.5% of the population, indicating a high dependency rate. While only about 4% of this force was female, mainly within the Amman urban region, female employment, with government encouragement, is on the increase.

Needless to say, the Jordanian labor market has witnessed a great deal of work specialization in recent decades, reflecting the great changes in lifestyles, income, and the general thrust of development. By and large, the labor force is disciplined and amenable to acquiring new skills and ideas. With urbanization reaching as high as 68.3% of the total population, there has also been a marked increase in the literacy rate, which is about 70%. All these shifts in population domicile, ways of making a living and education were to a large extent done with the government playing a major role in initiating, directing, and financing them. The welfare state is also a characteristic of Jordan, with the government now attempting to raise the standard of living and improve the quality of life for its young population, about 52% of which are under 15 years of age, and around 30% of which are in schools and training institutions. In the 1978/1979 school year, there were 670,290 students and 25,552 teachers in all types of schools, ranging from kindergarten to training, vocational and specialized institutes. The marked increase in the education of females has been one of Jordan's sources of pride in the last few years.

In 1978, there were 31 hospitals with 2,581 hospital beds. Three were also 66 health centers, 78 city clinics, 281 village clinics, 53 maternity and childcare centers, 1,106 physicians and 241 dentists.

Daily water consumption per person averaged 37.2 liters, markedly below the 150 liters considered to be the international standard. For Jordan, however, and in terms of its distribution and hygiene, it is a long step in the right direction. Also, an improvement in the availability and better distribution of electricity saw 78.3% of the population having access to it in 1979.

These are cold statistics and facts that tell everything and nothing at the same time. Traditions, customs, and old ways die hard and in stages, if they die at all. For there is a lot of individuality in what human beings do, and Jordan's population now has a highly individualistic middle-class mentality. Do these statistics tell us about the small shopkeeper, whose shop contains a vast array of often unrelated items? Or do they give the live atmosphere of an individual shoemaker, literally fashioning every shoe to please a customer? Our *Suks*, bazaars, markets and shopping centers still maintain an air of medievalism about them: the sound and smell of a bargaining, bustling, alive meeting place of shoppers and vendors reaching compromises. Every sale, no matter how small, is a deal, and we enjoy each sale, making it a personal affair between buyer and seller. Every sale carries with it its own excitement, and the personal touch is maintained. Relationships are weakened or strengthened at that time between the parties involved. You feel your cloth, your tomatoes, or bananas. Is the texture, right? Does it look good? And will it do? And you relate to the shop, the salesman and the product.

The *dukkan*, the shop, is small, less than three by five meters in most cases. There are more than a few customers jostling and touching each other, trying to get at the same goods at the same time. No one minds, and the owner is talking with everybody at the same time, gesturing, swearing oaths and trying to please. He is full of smiles.

Everything is personal; there is no anonymity. Even in larger private enterprises and government offices, the personal touch is maintained, often at the expense of efficiency and income. You do not fire Musa because he has seven children, and you tolerate the horrible and inefficient typing of Salmah because one day she will learn … you hope.

Our businessmen are not yet used to the idea of mass consumer market that is slowly but surely developing. That is why they insist on getting large margins of profit from small numbers of sales. They want to get the sale over and done with as quickly as possible, and in only very few cases or places is the customer allowed to return or exchange an item that he has purchased. Frequently the customer is very upset and angry; words are exchanged. In many shops and firms, signs are displayed cautioning customers that once the goods leave the premises the sale is final and no exchange is allowed.

The lingering emphasis on small-sale-large-profits is aggravated further by the general lack of credit offered to customers. Until quite recently, and even now in most cases, very few firms extend credit to their customers, or allow them to buy on an installment plan. Now this is slowly changing, though one frequently encounters signs hung, especially in smaller enterprises, stating that the firm does not allow any business on credit. The sign may run something like this: "Please forgive us and please do not blame us, but we cannot extend credit". Doing business with cash, coupled with lack of advertising, is still a major restriction on commercial activity. People still depend on personal acquaintances and knowledge in advertising their business. Even in the larger family-run enterprises, the personal touch is still maintained, and indeed expected. Even when some business firms or banks agree to extend credit, they usually insist on at least one, and in most cases, two well-known co-signers, which often makes it very difficult for people most in need of credit to get it.

And life goes on always a bit less efficiently than it ought to, but always more personal and human. Government employees the world over love to read their paper over many cups of coffee. This is also true in Jordan. Many a prime minister and decision maker has attempted to change this, only to give in finally because they, too, are cut from the same cloth. In their heart, they are the same, and no matter how they attempt to rise above it, to isolate themselves with efficiency, they just cannot do it.

People talk to you. The taxi driver strikes up a conversation and before he drives two kilometers, he has already found out all your vital statistics and personal information. He stores that handy information, and relates to it. On the sides of his taxi or truck he has painted birds, flowers, or animals he knows. More often, most of the time with a flourish, he has printed popular sayings, religious exhortations, poems, or dedications. I have always wondered why; and always hoped, as I still do, to go around and collect these bits of wit and wisdom for myself and posterity. Perhaps the driver or the machine operator wants to relate to this cold and very efficient piece of working metal. He wants to make it part of his life. He cannot scratch it behind the ear like he used to do with his horse, camel, or mule, nor can he feed it sugar. Is it his attempt to relate it to something familiar that he knows and understands? Or is it that our people are terrified and are constantly in need of protection from evil forces they cannot grasp ... the evil eye, or djinn ... and thus the need for amulets, religious protection, or something familiar?

Everywhere people talk to you. Even if they know they will never see you again, they would still like to chat. In some cases, they do not have the time, but they have the inclination. In the shop you are buying a radio, a pair of shoes, under-wear, or tomatoes, the salesman is incessantly talking and exhorting, and very soon the next customer chimes in and he, too, indicates his appreciation, or lack of it, for an item you have picked. At times he gets upset if you do not buy what he recommends.

In the office, factory, or enterprise, a spirit of mutual concern pervades. Everybody knows the intimate details of everyone else's life, style, income, aches, pains, and pleasures. The owner or the manager behaves in a very personal manner, very much as a father. If he is old, has a sense of humor and some natural talent for administrative skills, he will do very well. You do not strike against the firm because you are ashamed of Abu Ahmad the *mudeer*, the manager. You work very well today because Abu Ahmad was extra gentle or because for one reason or another he asked you to do so. . Should there be a misunderstanding or a fight between the two, everyone interferes or intercedes on behalf of the weaker party; a compromise is reached, dignity is maintained, the cheeks of both parties are kissed and things go back to normal, or what resembles normal. No hatreds or vendettas last very long and everyone is priding himself on and boasting of how "clean" his heart is, how he holds no grudges. Such a person is said to have a heart as pure as *laban*, yoghurt.

Life maintains an easygoing pace even in the worst circumstances. The boss wants very badly that something be completed by 2 o'clock, and he is bribing or cajoling, as the case may be. He has to deliver to someone else, who in turn has to deliver elsewhere. Two o'clock comes and goes, two days pass, and finally the work is done. He is very upset; so are those with whom he has had to deal, as are the third and fourth parties, each in their turn. Word is passed around that what happened should not have happened, but it did. What can one do? And everyone shakes his head with understanding. The tempo is relaxed and there is no terrific rush to catch up, although people are slowly learning how to respect time, and to budget it and to use it better.

But a tempo there is. The beat may not come with the precise regularity it does in the more efficient Western cultures, but a beat is there. Sometimes it is very strong, sometimes weak and irregular, but most always it holds surprises. An understanding of the weaknesses and frailties of human nature when and where least expected.

If your employee, your partner or your clerk or servant makes a mistake, damages the goods, or even steals a little, you are most likely to shrug it off. Sometimes you complain that the person is good but unfortunately "his hand is too long", meaning he steals a little and you have to watch him. And you do, and he steals, and you still watch, often missing it when he does not. The boiling point and the level of tolerance are exceedingly high and only in major scandalous or notorious cases of theft or bribery does anything happen. In fact, even then people understand and shake their head wisely muttering: "He is not the last one in the world to be bribed". If the punishment is severe, sympathy and understanding are with the culprit.

Corporal punishment, perhaps once practiced on a very limited scale, is very much despised and hated. Violence identifies the person as a harsh, severe and heartless person with whom no one likes to deal; it is exceedingly rare. A smile is always valued and more often than not it is not that dry, efficient, impersonal smile of "what can I do for you, sir?", but a personal one and almost a compliment to you. A person is valued if he smiles, and people extol this as a virtue, saying that "a smile never leaves his face!"

The social and cultural heritage has oiled the joints of human relationships to a point of fine tuning, with emphasis on avoiding negative friction and intercourse. If it does not work, or if a man is in a nasty mood, leave him now, come back tomorrow. And when two people are talking or dealing with each other, the conversation is replete with tidbits of wisdom, popular sayings and religious citations, all designed to take out the negative edge, to smooth out a situation or to gloss over a nasty affair. A situation has to be related to something else, and it is a rare Jordanian who cannot relate any situation to any-thing and, in a fantastic variety of ways. That is why they resort to how it was done in the old days; or, if generosity of pocket or heart is required, to some famous prophet or personage. Always invoking the name of God and citing religious verses or sayings is meant to create the proper atmosphere.

To others, I am sure this looks much like a waste of time or, perhaps, projects a sense of fatalism. In fact, it is related to human existence itself and its attempt at reaching as harmonious a relationship as is humanly possible. For, if the situation is negative, and you do not want to rub the other party the wrong way, you tell a parable, a story, a saying, indicating how it was done at other times and in other places. It is not simply to maintain and keep face, it is deeper than that. It is because you feel embarrassed in the presence of an embarrassing situation, and because you do not wish to expose this *Aib*, this shame, or mistake. Shame can take many forms and it is a chivalrous person who covers it. *Al-Tasatur*, covering a particular fault, is requited of people. One has to turn away when a woman is breast-feeding her child. That is a holy and beautiful task she is doing, and no man's eyes are allowed to look. *Al-Sutrah*, covering-up, is a concept that is not just to gloss over things; it is a recognition that one's faults, a family's fault or shame is a person's affair only, and no uninvited person should look into it or discuss it. Sometimes, when a person gossips, he will be told, "no … let it be covered, may God keep your shame covered". This is not hypocrisy. It is a realization that no human being alive, or who has ever lived, is without fault.

Surely, we often carry the concept of shame, or *Sutrah*, to the extreme, abusing a concept designed to make life more palatable and harmonious. But these situations are proper in the context of our cultural heritage that insists on close human relationships and personal touch.

Thus, whether it is in business, at a café or home, a person has to behave in a rather prescribed manner, by a set of rules for etiquette and proper behavior couched in a language designed to smooth out the rough edges.

It did not always go so smoothly, though, for there are a number of negative values that have emerged over centuries of repression, backwardness and instability, negative values that government and schools are now trying to overcome. A certain "lawlessness" of the self, individualism carried to the extreme emerged. These negative values, undisciplined for a long time by lack of central authority, whether moral or political, reflected themselves in many walks of life, including public and economic life. A company was often so specific to a family that it would call itself "the company of Ahmad and his brother Mustafa" not the company of "Ahmad and Brothers". Family-owned and operated most of the time, such company would often run inefficiently. This atomization of the economic life, inefficient as it was, did not leave room for large partnerships, public companies or corporations. These only began to emerge recently. Initiative and risk-taking, or long-term investment, did not reappear until well into this century.

The government, long viewed as, at best, only a "policeman" to be feared, is trying very hard and often succeeding in changing that image. Its efforts are pervasive, ranging from the physical to the conceptual. While building highways and hospitals, it is also trying to recreate a sense of loyalty to public life and eradicate the sense of *incivicisme*, or the lack of civic spirit and responsibility that developed in the centuries of decadence. It is extolling manual labor and teamwork, and instilling a sense of social equity and justice. Thus, there is talk of how the merit system should replace the *wasta*, nepotism, and talk of respect to be accorded to the *sani'*, the artisan, instead of the *tajir*, the middleman. If you still appoint your cousin to a job, people may complain or criticize, but they understand.

The inducements to change these negative values are many. While there is some resistance, it is not terribly serious, and the government's evolutionary approach is bearing fruit. There is an awareness at popular and official levels that change is needed, that it must be induced rather than imposed, and that is not easy to switch overnight from a semi- primitive to a consumer society without problems.

Amman. 24th anniversary of Arab revolt, celebration, September 11, 1940. One of the Emir Abdullah's Circassian guards.
G. Eric and Edith Matson, American Colony (Jerusalem).
Photo Department. Library of Congress.
Restoration by Kelvin Bown. *Reawakening the Past*, 2012.

Bedouin life in Trans–Jordan. An array of coffee pots around the fire,
1930–1933.
G. Eric and Edith Matson, American Colony (Jerusalem).
Photo Department. Library of Congress.
Restoration by Kelvin Bown. *Reawakening the Past*, 2012.

Chapter Four

The Family and Occasions

Social life in Jordan centers around the family, which is a tight-knit fabric of intricate relationships and attachments. Since Jordan is an extension of the Muslim Arab culture, the characteristics of the Jordanian family are similar to those elsewhere in the Arab Muslim East. It used to be extended, and in some localities, especially in the desert and the village areas, it still is. However, urbanization, education and economic pressures have greatly changed the family structure so that in most cases it is a cellular unit with the *Hamulah*, or the *Asheereh*, the tribe, both meaning the much larger unit of the extended family, in the background. If anyone, especially in the urban areas, identifies with the extended family, it is only on certain rare occasions of marriage with someone from another family where the practice has been rendered mainly ceremonial or in some blood feuds. No longer can the extended family function as it used to as a closed social and economic unit.

The various smaller components of the extended family used to support each other in a variety of ways. Even larger dinner invitations to another extended family, or to an important notable, were a cooperative effort. That practice has almost disappeared, except perhaps in some rural areas. The main function left for the extended family now is in blood feuds, when collective responsibility and mutual protection are still invoked to the rule of *Khamsah*, the group of five. The *Khamsah* of a man embraces all his patrilineal relatives who are within five degrees of relationship. The popular philosophy behind this collective protection is that if a person holds a stick with his five fingers it is difficult to take it away from him. Even here, in its attempt to assert its legal authority, the government finally abolished the Tribal Law in 1975. However; and even with government knowledge, the practice continues, and almost daily one reads in the newspapers about a reconciliation between two families according to tribal custom and practice.

Descent in the family is patrilineal. That is, each man is identified as belonging to his father's family, not his mother's. Yet, in Jordan, the mother's family is also very important for identification, and people usually ask who your *Khal* is, or maternal uncle, instead of asking about your *Am*, paternal uncle. For, in a village, small town, and Bedouin areas, a man often marries a woman not for her beauty, erudition, or grace, or because he loves her, but because he hopes she will bear good, intelligent, and courageous children like their uncles, her brothers. The idea is best expressed in the popular saying "two thirds of the boy take after his *Khal*".

The Jordanian family, before urbanization, used to be patrilocal, meaning that when the young men married, they would reside with or near their father. Now, and even with the new circumstances, it is still not uncommon for rich fathers to build a house with separate apartments for his children and their families. The practice is more prevalent in the rural areas, having been rendered too difficult and expensive in urban areas.

The father plays a dominant role in the Jordanian family, and his image is that of a patriarch presiding over his family's affairs. Once, his authority was rarely even questioned and his judgments were final. Now, and especially in urban areas, the hold the father used to have is no longer maintained, although he is still generally accorded the deference that one gives to a minor deity. The mother exhorts the children: "Whatever you do, do not anger your father". In Arabic, he is often referred to as *Rabula'ilah*, or *Rabul usrah*, head of the family, although the word *Rab* in Arabic refers also to the Lord.

Tradition directs that women take a secondary role in the affairs of the family, although the mother is also referred to as *Rabatu al-dar* or *Sit al Bait*, head of the household. The woman takes pride in this role, of which she is usually very aware.

The marriage preference, and this custom still lingers even in urban areas, is for bint al-'Am, the daughter of your father's brother. Should that be impossible for any reason, the preference is to marry from among the numerous cousins on either the father's or the mother's side. This endogamy trait in the

Jordanian family is still widely accepted and practiced by all strata of society.

Although some Western writers still describe the Jordanian family as polygamous, with more than one wife, that practice has become a relic of the past, though to divorce and marry again is practiced.

As one of the most important social institutions, the family in Jordan, and indeed in the Arab world, plays the role of broker between the individual and the society. The family molds the personality of the individual, instills in him its values, traditions, and ways of doing things, and despite the depth and breadth of the change taking place, determines a person's future behavior and course of life.

The Jordanian family is not like the family in the West, where children beyond the age of 18 or 20 are expected to grow out of it and leave it. You may hate your family, but very few ever leave its hierarchical mental or physical premises. One is never unattached to it, and very few people ever grow out of it. In Arabic, a man without a family is likened to a limb cut from a tree. Buttressed by religious and popular sayings and exhortations, the family's hold on an individual's life is difficult to describe. Even now, and in spite of the process of education and change, the cellular family still maintains its stronghold. The extended family still does in some cases, though to a much lesser degree. For the concept of the family is holy, and one is expected to do anything to protect, honor or defend it by whatever means are at hand.

Some social analysts, both Arab and non-Arab, have found fault with the workings, structure, and value-instilling process of the Arab family. Professor Hisham Sharabi, for instance, states categorically that it instills in the child a sense of dependency, lack of self-reliance and self-esteem, weakness of character, shame and guilt feelings. The criticism would have been more valid had our society placed its emphasis on values of aggression, combativeness, competition and isolated self-reliance where each man is an island unto himself, as is the case in American society. The comparison is not only unfair, it also negates a whole set of values that we happen to find positive. To be ashamed of a misdeed is something we find good, as it is to emphasize harmony instead of competition. Again, we find it reasonable to compromise and the mother's injunction that "when your father comes home, he will deal with the neighbor's boy who beat you" is an attempt at reconciliation and compromise. She knows that the father will talk to his neighbor, who in turn will deal with his aggressive son. A compromise is reached here and both boys realize that theirs is not a solitary world, that there are norms and customs and ways of handling a situation, and that violent retaliation is not necessarily the only recourse one may have.

Again, some say the father is a tyrant whose children tend to hate him and identify more with the mother. To some extent, there is some truth in identification with the mother's side, because of her nature and role in a seemingly patriarchal family structure. Very often the mother is overprotective of her children and very passionate in expressing her love and cherishment of them. Since the father is expected to be the head of the house, the bread winner and the liaison with the outside world (a man with many functions), he projects a certain distance between himself and the children. He comes home tired in the evening, and the mother exhorts her children to grant him comfort. The relationship between mother and father seems to be that of an inferior to a superior. That is how it looks to the outside world, although I have grown to suspect that the mother cultivates that image deliberately, since it helps her to maintain her hold on the children, and releases her from the burden of making her decisions public. To the outside world she knows, it is a compliment to her and to her husband if he appears to be the absolute boss. Thus, she allows him to be a bit gruff and even fosters that image. He, in turn, enjoys the role, and projects a strict and correct demeanor. He cannot appear too gentle, there is no display of affection, no holding of hands or kissing is allowed in public or in front of the children.

The father, for his part, protects the family, and in his relationship with the mother he always tries to be correct, in front of others, where he emphasizes that he does his duties, *wajibat*, and within the family, with the children. Here, and in most domestic cases, he defers to her judgment, and if the children ask permission to go someplace or do something, he invariably tells them "if your mother has agreed", or "if um Fahd, the mother of Fahd, agrees". Um Fahd is his wife, and it is customary that the man will refer to his wife in such a form, usually the name of his eldest son. She, in turn, refers to him as *Abu Fahd*, father of Fahd, even to her children. Very often, and to show respect to each other or to formalize a relationship, they will refer to each other as *Ibn* or *Bint 'Ami*, cousin, even though they are not related at all, the idea being that if she or he are cousins, they are equals.

By allowing the father to look like the traditional patriarch, some mothers often affect the aspect of a martyr who has sacrificed her life. If she has several children and is of middle age or above, very soon she acquires the resigned look of martyrdom and weariness. She begins to cultivate the image of being religious, constantly citing religious sayings and proverbs, and may even sigh a lot to punctuate her sentences. All of this is designed to appear in contrast to the aggressive father who might understand what is going on but who tolerates it, nonetheless. The cult of the mother thus develops with the sympathy of the children pouring in her direction. It helps her, when she grows older, to get fat because that enhances her helplessness. Her children are constantly reminded by her, and even by the father, how she "sacrificed her life for them", and the children are never free of that secret feeling of guilt that they are so obligated they can never do enough for her.

Whether the above description, or my feelings of the dynamic relationships between father and mother, is a defense of the father or an indication of the very central and important role the mother plays, it is difficult to tell. The point is that the mother's position is exceedingly secure, her rights sacrosanct, and she is respected, loved, and honored by her family. This is very important to emphasize, for very often one finds reference to the inferior role and status of women, even in the home. Far from it. In most cases, she is consulted on everything, whether within her "little kingdom", the home, or in the family's affairs, on all sorts of issue, whether economic or social. In all these affairs, her opinion is crucial, and often final. She helps in deciding her sons' and daughters' marriages, and hardly any affair is commenced or completed without her participation. Her maternal influence over her children is indeed very strong, and it is she, in most cases, who keeps the family's cohesion and gives it direction.

It is difficult, if not impossible, to catalogue the intricacies of family life, family relationships and dynamics. Yet it is important to attempt to project as close a picture as possible of the inner workings of the average Jordanian family. Nevertheless, the moods, the daily ups and downs, the pleasures and failures, minor fights over little nothings are hard to capture. There is love in the family. There is mutual concern. And often over-protectiveness. Often the children are so smothered with love they never grow up and continue to hearken back to the time "in our old house … with my mother"!

The extended family composed of first, second and distant cousins is an outer circle of relationships that an individual has. You may quarrel with your family or your cousins, yet to the outside world you maintain solidarity with them, thus adhering to two popular sayings: "My brothers and I against our cousins, and our cousins and us against strangers". If you give the job to your cousin, though his qualifications are less; "nepotism", people try to understand and tolerate, though they may not like the end result. This practice is getting less frequent due to the spreading emphasis on education and the emergence of the merit system.

The upbringing of the children is the prime concern of the father, mother, and adult members of the family. There is a conscious, as well as a subconscious effort at instilling conformity in the child. He is encouraged to act in a prescribed manner, and not to deviate too much from that prescription. He is constantly reminded of who he is, who his father is, and who his family is. He is reminded of how things were done by his grandfather and his ancestors, and is told he is to carry on in the same way in the future. The child, boy or girl, is encouraged to be gentle, respectful of elders and not too naughty. The ideal child, the popular saying goes, is the one you see but cannot hear. Almost always extra care is given to the male child, though the daughter, in most cases, is not neglected. When the boy is around eight or nine, the father begins to take him around with him. The daughter stays home with her mother and her feminine process of acculturation commences early, with visits to relatives, neighbors, and friends.

Father and mother talk to their children, of course, though there are exceptions. Both try to install in the child a sense of belonging that is sometimes too comforting. Talks may cover a variety of topics and directions, but almost always discussion of sexual matters is avoided. These matters, especially for boys, are learned in secret, with his peers in school or in the street. For girls, there is usually more discussion between mother and daughter, or between daughters and aunts.

Sexual discussions or reference to sexual matters are avoided within the family. The topic is wrapped in various veils of mystery, and the children are taught to avoid mentioning it or discussing it with anyone. *Hishmeh*, modesty, is highly valued in both males and females, and a mark of a modest person is that he never discusses sex. The child has to discover, as best he can, his knowledge about sex. Polite people never speak of or expose an *'Ourah*, pudenda, genitals or private parts. In fact, it is religiously enjoined that no such parts be exposed or discussed. People are asked to cover-up, *Yastru al-'Ourah*. Incidentally, popular parlance, especially among the less educated and poorer classes, refers to a woman also as an *'Ourah*, although even here change is taking place. A person who talks or attempts to talk about sexual matters openly is referred to as *qalil al-haya, "has little shame". As a result, sexual segregation is still one of the features of Jor*dan's society, though change is taking place here, especially in middle- and upper-class families in the urban areas.

Just as modesty is highly valued in both males and females, virginity is very much emphasized and promiscuity is frowned upon. A virgin is more valuable, and tragedies often occur when on the wedding night a girl is thought or discovered not to be a virgin, often leading to a long and protracted blood feud involving the honor of both families. A woman who is shy or gives that impression is very highly appreciated and extolled.

Romantic love takes place and Arabic poetry and tradition are replete with passionate love stories, very often tragedies that would make the tragedy of Romeo and Juliette pale by comparison. Romantic love emphasizes a very clean and asexual affair, with the whole business almost from the beginning bordering on tragedy, and almost always ending in it. This tradition pre-dates Islam and has roots in Biblical times. Remember *sayyidnah Ya'koub*, our Master Jacob, who had to work seven years and then another seven to get his beloved Leah? *Al-hub al'uthri*, romantic asexual love, is very highly appreciated, and because of the veritable segregation of the sexes, it is practiced by almost everyone who is not married and under the age of 25. Ironically enough, sex is more relaxed in Bedouin culture, where an admirer may visit his beloved, spend time with her unchaperoned, and all with the knowledge of the girl's family. Such a situation is not tolerated in towns, cities and villages, where only if one is formally engaged can he visit his fiancée; even then, custom demands that they have a chaperon.

Licit sexual activity is almost a sacred duty in our society, with young men being admonished to complete "the other half of their religion". That is, they are encouraged to get married and have children. Illicit sexual behavior is frowned upon, although the reprobation is stronger in the case of a promiscuous woman. It is tolerated more, understood and even, in some cases, extolled in men, thus giving a double standard to sexual behavior.

Because of the extra care given to the boy, the girl tends to fend for herself and learns earlier how to become self-reliant. In most cases, girls are more resourceful than boys in handling situations. Another reason for this, no doubt, is the fact that the girl is constantly reminded by being addressed as an "Aroos", a bride, and that one day she will leave her father's house. She is often referred to as a guest in her father's house, and the father and brothers are thus exhorted to treat her well, since she is a guest.

On the whole, children are loved, and abuse or severe corporal punishment is frowned upon, though it is still practiced. Children are considered a blessing and at the same time one of the most important pleasures of this life. Men are enjoined to have more children and to be "fruitful and to multiply". Remember, God blessed *Abuna Ibrahim Khalilulal*, our father Abraham, friend of God, with children.

On the popular level, the belief that corporal punishment is necessary still lingers on with the popular saying "the stick is from Heaven", though you hear many people these days priding themselves that they have never beaten their children. Schools, newspapers and government radio and television programs are constantly debating the issue and preaching against corporal punishment.

One of the happiest family occasions is when a child is born, especially a male child. If the father is not present, someone is sent to tell him the good news and the messenger is given a present by the father for the *Bisharah*, the good tidings. The male child is usually named after his paternal grandfather, and the female after her maternal grandmother, although there are variations and deviations from this norm. The next happy occasion is the *Fitam*, the weaning of the child, whence his or her father will celebrate the occasion with food and often with singing and dancing. In Muslim families, the next occasion is the *Tuhur*, circumcision, literally relating to cleanliness. For the Christians, it is usually the baptism. In both cases dinner, singing, and dancing celebrate the occasion.

Nowadays, when a child graduates from high school or college it is a joyous occasion celebrated by the entire family. Friends and relatives are united on all these occasions and usually they come bringing with them appropriate presents. The next happy affair in a person's life is his or her engagement. The affair is often prearranged and agreed to by the families of both parties, although on the appointed day everyone goes through the prescribed ritual as if no agreement had ever been reached before.

The *Khutbeh*, engagement, in both Muslim and Christian communities, is a serious and more elaborate affair than the wedding. The reason is that once an engagement is agreed to, it is difficult, rare and in some cases impossible to break. One does not engage *banat el-Nas*, "daughters of the people", haphazardly or playfully. It is a shame on the girl and her family to have her engagement fail. Usually the mothers agree, through intermediaries, or directly if they are relatives or friends.

Husbands are told, and their consent assured; the details are worked out by the mothers. The boy visits his future in-laws prior to the formal ceremony, where in most cases he "accidently" runs into his future fiancée and learns to talk to her. Acceptance assured by both parties, the formal engagement ritual commences. A *Jahah*, a delegation of the boy's family plus some notables and dignitaries, proceeds on an agreed-upon date to the girl's house and formally asks for her hand. Here, in Muslim families, details concerning the amount of the dowry, *Mutaqadim* (pre-payment) and *Mutaakhir* (post-payment) should the marriage one day fail, are worked out. Also worked out are the details of the marriage ceremony, the bride's trousseau, her jewelry and all the rest.

It is a jubilant occasion, with the formalities taking only a small part of the time. The girl's family on this occasion has prepared a feast of fine foods and delicacies. Much singing, dancing, and clapping of the hands goes on.

The marriage date is usually agreed upon by both the bride and groom. The ceremony is a simple one, with the cost of festivities this time borne by the groom and his family. When the wedding date arrives, the bride is carried to her future husband in a ceremony called the *Zaffeh*. In rural areas, the bride is literally carried on horse or camel-back with much singing dancing and firearm shooting. The wedding ceremony for Muslims is a very simple one, usually followed by another feast of eating, singing, and dancing. And life goes on!

Sickness is a sad occasion, with relatives and friends visiting the invalid at home or in the hospital, as the case may be. Usually, the visitors bring with them presents of fruits, flowers, or chocolates, or give money to help cover some of the hospital expenses. The saddest occasion is death, which is considered part of life. Though very sad, our people have a strange philosophy concerning it. No-one likes to witness the death of a beloved one, but only on very rare occasions is anybody ever totally broken up over death. "We love uncle Khalil but it was God's will that he died … we cannot change that … death is a continuation and part of life…" It is to honor the dead if you can bury the deceased the same day or, in most cases, the next day. Though this indicates a healthy respect for his life, certain ceremonies have to be observed. The women must wear black; in the old days, for one or more years, but now, for no more than 40 days. Everyone is supposed to look sad, and not enjoy themselves, attend a cinema, wedding, or joyous occasion until the period of *Hidad*, mourning, has passed. Again, in the old days, this was a long period ranging from 40 days to two years; now it is observed for no more than 40 days by most people, unless the deceased is the husband. In this case, the wife is expected to wear black for at least a respectable one-year period.

Nowadays, death is usually announced on the radio and in the newspapers. In the last few years, an unhealthy new custom has developed in Jordan regarding these announcements, with the family and friends of the deceased outbidding each other in publishing personal announcements with pictures of the deceased in the obituary pages of the daily newspapers. This is very costly to the family and friends, and often puts a financial burden on them, such has become the intensity of this new form of social pressure. In the announcement, the separate places where men and woman may go to pay their respects and condolences is indicated. The *'Aza*, or period of condolence, is now customarily three days. In the old days, it was six months, 40 days, or two weeks, depending on the wealth and importance of the deceased. The immediate family of the deceased who are present are fed, and friends or members of the family usually bring cooked food from their home or, now, order it from restaurants.

Men created these customs and men adhere to them with such punctiliousness and faithfulness it touches the heart. Surely it brings us back to an earlier realization that people tend to create their own myths, as well as realities, and adhere to both with tenacity.

The Jordanian people, though changing their ways of life radically, still cling to certain customs and traditions. The move to the city, wearing of city clothes and the outward manner- isms have not completely replaced the old ways. Now wearing trousers instead of the substantial *Sirwal*, or a jacket in place of the old *Damer*, they still maintain some of the old customs. These outward changes have not swept away everything before them. The women in the villages used to, as some still do, wear a hand-embroidered *Shursh*, a dress with a graceful cut. This was accented by a hand-woven *'asbeh*, a scarf on her head, and silver jewelry to fit different occasions. Among the customs is the celebration of all occasions with food. Births, baptisms or circumcisions, birthdays (now that some of the affluent celebrate them in the cities), engagements, marriages, the departure or the arrival of a loved one, honoring friends, parents or relatives and almost every other human activity are celebrated with food. People find or look for any excuse to get together over a meal and to feast. For Jordanians, it is enough to get together, and the food is often the excuse. People eat with joy and pleasure. To break bread and salt, *Aish Wa Milih*, with someone else is to seal a friendship with something almost ritually sacred, and not just simply to eat; for eating is considered a private affair. One eats with joy and relaxation only with friends and loved ones. That is why until quite recently it was considered bad form for people to eat in restaurants. Only people who have no family or friends were unfortunate enough to have to eat in restaurants. Now, that too is changing.

On big occasions, Jordanians cook *Mansaf*, our delicious national dish made of lamb cooked in yoghurt sauce and served on a large tray lined with *shrak*, a kind of flat bread, and heaped with rice and piled with the lamb chunks and yoghurt sauce poured on top, garnished with roasted almonds, pine nuts and parsley, traditionally served with green onions and radishes. The Palestinians often cook their national dish of *Musakhan*, chicken roasted in olive oil with diced onions heartily sprinkled with sumac served over *Taboun*, flat bread.

Is it possible to tell about a people by the way they eat? The Jordanians think eating is a private affair, to be enjoyed with friends, and thus many are still nervous eating in restaurants with waiters and other patrons. When finishing, it is expected to thank your host and wish him well, to say *al-hamdulillah*, thank God, several times. It is almost a ritual.

Jordanian cuisine is, of course, an extension of Arab cuisine, and contrary to some opinions, very little spice is used, with salt, pepper and cinnamon being the most common. The food is not very rich, and is usually served hot with much of the meal consisting of stuffed vegetables. The Arabs stuff grape leaves, cabbage, and many other leafy vegetables. Usually, they hollow out vegetables such as squash, potatoes, tomatoes, onions and egg plants, stuff them with a mixture of delicately flavored minced meat and rice and cook them. The cuisine is varied, aromatic and delicious.

Bedouin woman baking bread, 1900–1920.
G. Eric and Edith Matson, American Colony (Jerusalem).
Photo Department. Library of Congress.
Restoration by Kelvin Bown. *Reawakening the Past.*, 2013.

Bedouin of Adwan tribe. at Shunet Nimrin, etc., April 25, 1935.
G. Eric and Edith Matson, American Colony (Jerusalem). Photo
Department. Library of Congress.
Restoration by Kelvin Bown. *Reawakening the Past*, 2016.

Chapter Five

Culture

Like an old house that has known much living, Jordan has developed a sense of diversity and openness about it. If it has learned anything since the dawn of modern history, it has learned to accept almost anything. To accept, not tolerate, for the latter carries the feeling that one is suffering from an obnoxious sight, sound, or smell. Acceptance is a deeper concept, perhaps more prejudiced at times, but certainly more human. You accept, not tolerate, your neighbor's mores, abnormalities, and habits though you may not like them. For tolerance carries with it the idea that one day you may no longer tolerate. This is one reason for the beauty and diversity of the Arab Middle Eastern cultural mosaic. If you value things, you value them for whatever you think they are worth, but never because you think you should suffer to value them. You may disagree with them or even dislike them, but you grant others the right to be different if that is what they want.

The Jordanians are preoccupied with life. Individually, they are, or have become, open-minded, quick to imitate and to appreciate, with many new ideas eventually taking hold. This is not just a Jordanian trait; it is, in fact, an Arab, indeed, a Muslim trait that has marked Muslim culture to be not only highly versatile and diversified, but always amenable to accepting new ways and methods, regardless of the place or the time. Soon Yugoslav, Pakistani, or Indonesian folklore becomes part and parcel of the Muslim heritage, and still sooner it is accepted by even the general public as a new and welcome additional Islamic stream, and one that people are proud of.

Culturally, our people waver between what is and what was. The past, glorious as it was, rightly holds its own attractions, but the future has just as strong, and limitless, attractions. A person's soul is torn between all these possibilities and probabilities. That is why it is not uncommon to find several cultural personalities in the same person. The mood may be Oriental, Western, or somewhere in-between, and one is responsive to all these moods, not out of blind or superficial imitation, but because of a genuine appreciation of both the traditional and the new. And it is thus that every Jordanian lives in a variety of worlds … old, new and in-between. The choice and diversity is bewildering, and rich.

The average urban Arab or Jordanian has learned to appreciate Um Kalthoum and modern Western music. His taste includes an appreciation for the gyrating movements of the belly dancer and her modern choreographic rival on the modern stage. The average Jordanian has become acquainted with other cultures, principally the Western culture, and has learned to appreciate it next to his own.

Jordan is an extension of the surrounding Arab culture. In a way, it is part and parcel of that culture, and thus difficult to be distinguished from it, except for the very discriminating the discerning. Yet, in fact, local variants do exist, and Jordan has succeeded in identifying certain cultural themes that are similar to, yet distinct from, the stream of Arab cultures surrounding it. Its situation, and perhaps that of surrounding countries, is similar to that of, say, Mississippi or Tennessee in the general stream of American culture, or that of Scotland or Wales in British culture, an enriching stream that nonetheless can claim a certain distinction. In Jordan's case, that distinction is further enhanced by the presence of the Palestinians as part of this stream. In the last two decades, there has been an attempt at "reviving" or rather asserting a Jordanian identity. Since 1970, this assertion of Jordanianism has accelerated, no doubt out of fear of losing one's identity. This revival is seen in folk dancing, music, clothing, and other aspects of life.

As part of the Middle Eastern culture, Jordan has also become a racial, but certainly not a cultural, melting pot. Assyrians still enjoy their own food and music from ancient times, Circassians enjoy the *Fantasia* dance they brought with them, and Turkmen or Gypsies enjoy their own food and habits in the accepting cultural atmosphere of Jordan. That is why all have survived. In Christian churches, chants and music of 1,000 or 1,500 years ago are still sung and enjoyed. People may not understand the ceremony in a Greek Orthodox

Church, but they will nonetheless accept and even enjoy it, since it has become part of the culture.

Craftsmanship and Folklore

Craftsmanship has never died in Jordan, as indeed it has not died elsewhere in the Muslim world. Craftsmen of various skills inherited from their fathers the ability to make earthenware jars, vases, jewelry, glass work, metalwork, leather work, weaving, glazed pottery, wood-inlay, tapestry, *busut* (striped woolen rugs), embroidery, shell work and engraving. Tinned brass and copper-wear are made for use as cooking and eating utensils, and often also artifacts for decoration. Other crafts include woodwork, hand-blown glass, wrought-iron work and silver and gold jewelry; bead work, straw and rattan, embroidery and stone cutting. Local material was used, and the products were sold to and appreciated by all strata of the population, and not just the privileged few. While the product was beautiful, there was also very little innovation or variation on a particular pattern or theme. An earring, a tapestry, a rug, or a brass pot were made in a certain pattern, and rarely was any innovation made. The creation of a new artistic effect, or a new style, was very rare indeed. The emphasis was always on adhering to a particular pattern or theme. This conservatism and quietism in artistic expression had no room for the emergence of renowned, great artists, art being decorative rather than representative. The pattern may vary slightly from village to village, or among the Bedouins, but a pattern it remained that basically clung to the traditional design. In fact, even in clothing, a person who knows the pattern can still pinpoint to you the village or the area from whence a woman, and even a man, originates.

Painting

In the last few decades, artistic expression in the form of painting of the human form and in the Western tradition has become an accepted fact. Calligraphy, ornamental designs, and geometric ornamentation remain legitimate forms of artistic expression, but the rendering of the human body in representational painting has once again been revived in Jordan. Remember that it is only in Jordan, perhaps very few other places in the world, that the rendering of the human form by Islamic artists can be found. *Qasr Amrah*, Amrah palace, built about 715 AD in the Jordanian desert, is one of the very few Islamic places in the world depicting the human form. Its murals of dancers, musicians and hunting scenes are among the finest examples of early Islamic art relegated to misuse over centuries.

With government encouragement and with a growing audience in the urban areas, the painting tradition has been revived, and Jordan now has a number of good artists and painters. Kamal Boullata, Rafiq Laham, Laith Shammout, Suhail Bisharat, Farouk Lambaz, and Mohanna Durra, among others, are representatives of today's Jordanian artists. Representative of Jordan's women artists are Princess Wijdan, Samia Zaru,

Afaf Arafat, Princess Fakhr al-Nisa and Da'd al-Tell. Their themes are both local and international, traditional and modern. Mohanna Durra, in particular, has been exhibited several times in Jordan, Italy, Canada, Austria and the United States, and is a very highly appreciated artist in Jordan. His works may be found in the Vatican, the Imperial Court of Japan, Moscow State Museum, and many other venerable art institutions.

Sculpture has lagged somewhat behind painting, but even here, a number of good artists have developed. Kuram al-Nimri, Samer Taba', and Abdul Rahman Al-Masri are representative of Jordan's contemporary sculptors.

Music

It is a mark of the changing times that even in musical tastes there are now many changes. For music is highly private, and though its appreciation is often collective, it remains an inner and personal affair. At one time in the *Badia*, the desert areas, and in the rural countryside, almost every human activity had its own song or chant. Music was an integral part of life. Even today, and in the cities, it is not uncommon to hear men working in groups singing or chanting. There used to be songs for weddings and other religious occasions, ploughing and harvesting.

Urbanization has done away with much of that. Urbanization, and the influence of the cinema, the mass media, especially television. Television, while a boom to the arts, both audio and visual, is slowly replacing the diverse variety with a "national" theme. Radio, of course, has played and continues to play a big role in the process of homogenization. If any variety exists today, it is not that traditional variety of music attached to a locality; rather, it is a variety of tone, source and beat. One may listen, especially in the urban areas, to several types of music in the same household: a medley ranging from the traditional Bedouin or village music to the Western classical or popular music. One may hear the traditional music of the *ataba* and *mijana*, in which the modulating, ululating voice is enriched with meaningful lines of praise to a notable or to a loved one. All Jordanians enjoy this type at least occasionally. Next is the modern Arab music, both from Jordan and from other Arab countries. Songs of Um Kalthoum or Farid al-Atrash, Fahid Najjar and Tawfiq Nimri are enjoyed. They represent a blend between traditional and modern Arab musicology. A third type of music is ultra modern Arab music, which represents a mixture between an Arab theme and a Western melody. Typical of this is the music of Fairuz and that of the Bandali family. In the desert areas, Bedouin folk music takes, or rather used to take, basically two forms. The one called *al-Hujaini* was literally sung to the rhythm of the camel gait. It is often a lively form of singing performed at weddings and other joyous occasions. The second form, sung mostly to the accompaniment of the *Rababah*, an ancient one-string violin-like instrument, is called the *Shuruqy*. The themes tell of raids, battles, generosity or praise of one Shaikh or another. It often sounds very melancholy. Finally, one may find, especially among the young in urban areas, a growing audience for Western music, ranging from rock to the classical, symphonic and semi-classical themes.

Minorities in Jordan enjoy their own music, traditional chants and dances. Circassian music, in particular, has become part of Jordan's cultural heritage, with Cossack costumes and dances that are highly synchronized and expressive. The Circassian National Club organizes several festivals each year and Circassian music and dance are often featured on radio and television. Men and women dance together, yet like the Arab tradition, it is exceedingly rare for the dancers of different sexes to touch each other.

In addition to all of the above, one should not forget to mention religious music, sung on both Muslim and Christian occasions. The traditional rendering of the Holy Koran in song is very widely practiced on all occasions, whether joyous or sad. In fact, the call to prayer by the *Muazzin* is one of the most beautiful art forms of this type. In the various Christian churches, ancient tunes and chants have been preserved, often to the accompaniment of various musical instruments.

Jordanians like their music, and very often will find any excuse to enjoy it. It is not uncommon for a family or a circle of friends to start singing and clapping, often having a young boy or girl dance. This is done whether there is an occasion or not. Sometimes a family or friends on a ride in the car will start clapping and singing. Should the occasion be more formal, a *Durabakkeh*, drum is produced, and if that is not available, a cooking pot will do, and the singing and clapping commence.

On occasions, the *Oud*, lute, may be present, and it is the mark of a very good player to play *taqasim*, improvisations on a popular theme. In fact, not only is an individual player judged good if he improvises, but quite often, a whole *takht*, orchestra improvises together and, indeed, is expected to do so. This is also expected of the singer, who is supposed to respond to the mood of his audience and improvise as he goes along in his song. This is very much unlike Western music, written down and orchestrated so no deviation or improvisation whatsoever is allowed. The feeling is not for static art, but for dynamic spontaneity allowing for the freedom of self-expression of singers and musicians alike.

The *Nawar*, gypsies, are very much loved in Jordan for they have kept the tradition of singing and dancing alive and healthy. They play the *Rababah*, one string violin, or the *buzuk*, a long-necked mandolin-type instrument. Currently Jamil al-'As is credited with being the King of *Buzuk* in Jordan, and his services are very much in demand by the wealthy, as well as by the television and radio stations. Other popular instruments in Jordan include the *Nayy*, the flute, or the *Mijwiz*, two reeds next to each other, or the *Mizmar*, another type of flute. The *Qanun*, a very complicated and exceedingly melodious oriental harp-type instrument, is also present.

Dancing

Jordanian Palestinian music is an extension of, as well as, an integral part of Arab music enjoyed in Syria, Lebanon, Egypt or Saudi Arabia. There are local themes that have helped give it a certain flavor that one may call distinctly Jordanian, in the same sense that Western, hillbilly, or southern music in America is part of the American theme, though having a distinct flavor. Jordanians take pride in what they consider Jordanian music.

Jordanians love to dance. In fact, whenever a few individuals of both sexes are gathered together someplace, it is not unusual for them to begin singing and clapping. Soon they will coax somebody in the group to dance. Often it is only a little boy or girl. Later in the evening, and after many cups of tea, it might be a young lady, the beautiful wife or mother of one those present. The female gets up and soon someone will find a shawl which she ties around her hips, and dancing and partying commence with spirit. There is an easy-going and relaxed atmosphere within the family or among friends.

The *Dabkeh* is an elaborate line dance whereby several people, either men or women, or both, dance to the *Dal'ona* tune, a popular song. *Dabkeh* is a choreographed dance with a variety of steps, different from locality to locality. There is a lot of foot-work and timed stamping of feet. It has a variety of rhythms that distinguish the dance of one town from another. A lively form of dancing among the bedouins, which has almost become extinct is the *Sahjeh*. This form of dancing involves a group of men that may reach 20, who form a semicircle in the midst of which a beautiful girl, carrying a sword or knife and called the *Hashiah*, begins to dance to their singing, brandishing her sword in the middle of the circle of men. Very soon starts the *Dahhiyyah*, very fast clapping, usually accompanied by a throaty chant. The men are trying to touch the body of the *Hashiah*, who is keeping them at bay with her dagger or sword. So the lively contest-dance continues.

The people enjoy *Haz al-Batin*, belly dancing, and young boys or girls are often asked to perform it in a clean spirit of camaraderie and fun. It is not uncommon for a man in a group of men, or a girl or woman in a group of females, to dance alone. School boys or girls, whether in a bus going on a picnic or at a gathering, enjoy this form of entertainment, and young mothers are very proud when their small children can do the dance.

The Theater

The theaters of Jerash, Petra, Um Qais and Amman, among others, attest to a long tradition of theater in Jordan, one that has died in past centuries, not to be revived until modern times. Even when the theater literally died in Jordan, as indeed it did elsewhere in the Middle East, certain traditional theatrical performances persisted in one form or another. Among these were the shadow play, the *Argouz*, a Punch and Judy-type show, and *Sandouk al-Ajaib*, "box of miracles", or peep show. Theater in the modern sense was first revived in Egypt, from whence it spread to other Arab lands. In modern times, theatrical presentations in Jordan began in the late 1920s with high school plays, and mushroomed in a variety of ways to a semi-vigorous theatrical movement. The University of Jordan has become a major medium for this form of artistic expression, and its theatrical output is highly appreciated. Hani Snouber, Mahdi Yanis, Ashraf Abaza and Ahmad Qawadri are among the most prominent theatrical actors and producers at the same time. The Haya Art Center, headed by Nabil Sawalha, was established by government to develop children's artistic talents and appreciation in all areas of art, particularly the performing arts.

Theater, in spite of government encouragement, has remained the least developed of the performing arts. This is probably because of the terrific devotion needed on the part of the performers themselves, in addition to the fact that a vigorous theatrical taste needs to be developed further. Nor should it be forgotten that when theatrical performances began to reappear, television also appeared at the same time. Even countries with long theater traditions saw a decline in theater attendance due to this new, very available and con-venient source of entertainment.

Literature

The most vigorous and important form of artistic expression in Jordan is the word, both prose and poetry. Literature, in Arabic called *al-Adab*, carries with it a moral tone. To be an *adeeb*, litterateur, in Jordan means that one is basically developing a moral theme, a series of "nays" and "yays", themes that are often highly moralistic and at times disciplined to the point of being dull.

No form of artistic expression thrills the average Arab more than a decent piece of poetry or prose. Everybody, or almost everybody, enjoys listening to poetic renderings, "duelling" in poetry. *Al-Munazarah al-Shi'riyyeh*, "duelling" or a contest in poetry, is still a beautiful pastime especially for young people. It consists of showing-off which of the two teams or persons can recite more poetry. One person recites a verse and the other person has to recite a verse beginning with the last pronounced letter of the verse just completed; and it often goes on for hours at a time. It is not unusual for young high school or college students to be able to recite literally thousands of verses. A young Bedouin used to be taught poetry alongside fighting, even before reading and writing were stressed.

Our people enjoy our language immensely and a *fasih*, an eloquent person who has a knack for expressive speech, is much appreciated. He is said to have a way with words and, accordingly, is considered with esteem. In today's Jordan, indeed in the Arab world, three forms of our language have emerged: the classical language of the Holy Quran; the modern-day newspapers, or popular literature; and the local *Lahjeh*, dialect, which varies from locality to locality, and often from town to town.

Our people love to talk, often mistaking talking for action. Our seeming helplessness in dealing with the Zionist threat adds to our frustration, which seeks vent in the spoken or written word. The word becomes balm to the soul, and soon it acquires a strength all its own. It cleans one's soul and almost washes away one's sins. Sometimes I have the feeling that our people mistake expression for action, and that they feel that if they just express how they feel others will understand and injustice will be righted.

Poetry

In this century, Jordan has produced some very influential and good poets. King Abdullah himself was both a litterateur and a poet of accomplishment. His Friday *diwan*, salon, was well attended and he used to delight in examining those attending in the intricacies of our language. Mustafa Wahbeh al-Tell is perhaps the best known of Jordan's 20th century poets. He was renowned for his style, so very smooth and melodious, as well as for the social content of his poetry. He espoused the cause of the poor, the downtrodden and the underdog. His themes of Jordanian life and scenery and his espousal of and love for the gypsies singled him out as a poet of the masses, and not a palace poet. His escapades with King Abdullah, attacks on government, repentance, forgiveness by the King, and later attacks are told to this day with wonderment and adoration by many. Other accomplished poets include Abdul Monim Al-Rifai, twice prime minister of Jordan and a poet of classical form, taste and content. Thurayya Malhas, Fadwa Tuqan, Najwa Kawar Farah, Ibrahim Mustafa Zaid al-Kaylani, Muhammad Said al-Jundi, Khalid Nasra, Kamal Nasser, M.S. al-Afghan, and Abdul Rahim Omar; they are all well-known and accomplished poets whose styles and themes are both modern and traditional, frivolous and highly nationalistic or serious: Something to please everyone at all times!

In the last decade, a writers' union was formed and has been active in sponsoring and activating literary life in Jordan. Writers of novels, short stories, plays and poetry belong to it, and it has been receiving government support and help since its inception. Jordan has developed a number of prose writers of note: Rox ben Zaid al-Uzzaizi, with his highly stylistic historical writing and themes of Bedouin folklore; Issa Nauri, with his modern outreach into other cultures, principally Italian literature, Suleiman al-Musa, with his historical scholarly studies and the late Mahmoud al-Abidi are a few of the many of note. Tayseer Saboul, Mahmoud al-Samrah, Abdul Rahim Omar, Fawwaz Tuqan, Husni Fareez are others whose names have dominated the field in the last few years. King Abdullah's Memoirs and his grandson King Hussein's book *Uneasy Lies the Head* are among the major works of autobiographical literature. Needless to say, a complete catalogue is impossible to include, such has been the spread of the literary movement.

Role of Government

The role the government has played and continues to play is difficult to ascertain. It is certain, however, that government sponsorship and encouragement of the arts and artistic expression, whether written, oral, audio or visual, has had a large impact on Jordan's cultural life and development. In fact, without such government sponsorship and encouragement, it is doubtful that one would witness the vigor and spontaneity of the present state of the arts. This role is expected to develop further, for it is doubtful that the private sector can assume this role of patron, which brings us back to an earlier remark: art and artistic expression, the handicrafts in particular, have never been the privilege of the aristocratic or the rich few, but are enjoyed by the populace at large. It is government sponsorship of the arts which made the by-passing of any traditional Islamic injunction against the rendering of the human form less of an issue. No-one now cares to discuss the issue or even bring it up.

The ministries of information and culture have been given the task of fostering and encouraging the arts. Both ministries frequently sponsor or invite both local and foreign artists and performers to visit and exhibit in Jordan.

We live from revolution to revolution, or from one *coup d'état* to another, not just in the political realm, but in the socio-cultural and economic one as well. Innovation is not new to us, especially since the pace has become a gait, indeed, a fast run, and we have learned to love it as well as to live with it.

Concluding Remarks

Our art and our culture are contemplative and meditative. Perhaps the smoothness of the wind-swept land, though looking harsh in places, has something to do with it. You see, we do not like to clash with nature, and we are never harsh with it, partly because we love it and partly because we know that ultimately nature always wins. Thus, we have learned to harmonize with it. We have also learned that life is really not so organized. In fact, we have learned that life is often a series of accidents, and disorganized and unrelated events coming together in a theme of one form or another. We have learned not to judge or attempt to control nature, but to harmonize with it. Even the Romans, once they reached our land, learned to harmonize with nature. Witness the oval theater at Jerash, which is, in essence, an abandonment of the traditional straight line of Roman architecture.

This is because our nature is so harsh, essentially, and yet so gentle looking at the same time. Unlike the English, the French or the Swedes, we do not have to build against the elements. We build with them. We welcome draughts, and do not build against them; our winds are not freezing, nor are we afraid lest the roof may cave in from the weight of the snow. The desert is an open space that teaches its frequenter how insignificant he is next to it. Very soon, he becomes not only wordy or poetic, he also becomes metaphysical and learns not to fight nature. And nature is at once brutal, gentle and diverse.

Since one can never hope to understand it completely, nor to control it, one has to learn how to live with it on its own terms, and one learns how to sublimate things. Realism renders things material and harsh, and leads to death. That is why you never have the urge to eat an apple or a pear painted by an Arab artist. You feel more like contemplating it.

Even when we build, we build in a medley of colors, materials, and styles. Ours is an accepting culture that appreciates diversity and sees no contradiction in it. Just look at the *Khazneh*, the Treasury building in Petra, where you find several styles in the same building, all giving a pleasant effect, seemingly unrelated, and maybe psychedelic and clashing to some, yet blending together in a harmonious theme, a mosaic. There you will see the strong and very well pronounced Greek-Hellenistic triangle, the slanted lines of ancient Egyptian building, the three stepped Assyrian *Ziggurat* and the Nabataean Arab Oriental circle and arch, all coexisting side by side to give a total effect that is pleasant to the eye.

Amman, and Jordan's modern building and design, still exhibit the same diversity and variety. The unique architecture is an example of the harmony that one finds in diversity. Its unifying theme is the medium, the material: the limestone of various shades of white, ever so versatile and beautiful. Like the buildings of old, the modern buildings and homes of Amman have many windows and doors; is this to bring the outside in or to take the inside out? I do not know, but the effect is of a certain sense of openness and spaciousness. Perhaps it is a carryover from the harsher desert times, when generosity to friend, neighbor and wayfarer was not kindness, but duty. Is that why our homes have a *Liwan*, a special family living room, and a *diwan*, a guest room, the latter always kept tidy to receive guests, friends and visitors? It seems we always intend to receive friends and visitors.

Woman weaving a straw mat. Semi Bedouin type in M'Keis, ancient
Gadara, 1920–33.
G. Eric and Edith Matson, American Colony (Jerusalem). Photo
Department. Library of Congress.
Restoration by Kelvin Bown. *Reawakening the Past*, 2015.

Petra. Khazne from S.E, 1940–46.
G. Eric and Edith Matson, American Colony (Jerusalem).
Photo Department. Library of Congress.
Restoration by Kelvin Bown. *Reawakening the Past*, 2014.

Chapter Six

Politics: Hussein and the Modern Hashemites

Jordan's is not a totalitarian regime, nor is it a dictatorship. Attempting to catch up with the times, it has developed a welfare state at a breathtaking pace. The arm of the welfare state is everywhere, its activities are felt in every aspect of human life. Responding to the vicissitudes of the time, its political development was often not only retarded, but, at times, even arrested. Both internal and external factors had something to do with this. Since 1921, there has been an attempt at making the Western-type parliamentary system work. That attempt was at first thwarted by the constant interference of the British authorities, and in 1928 an Organic Law was finally allowed to pass, providing for a much-reduced assembly called the Legislative Council, chosen by a cumbersome system of indirect elections. Five such Legislative Councils were elected between 1929 and 1942. Following the termination of World War II, and in response to the constant agitation for a more liberal constitution and a more meaningful representative body, the first *Majlis Al-Ummah*, or Parliament, was elected in 1947. King Abdullah I, greatly influenced by the Ottoman compromising school and sensitive to the times, was not averse either in principle or in practice to the idea of further liberalization. While the turmoil and anger that marked the 1950s had not yet touched Jordan, the country was politically "manageable", and given time, it might develop constitutionalism and its political institutions as well. The King, who was also very aware of the developments in the area, especially in Syria, must have felt that a participatory democratic system would enhance Jordan's image. Believing in evolution, he thought the new parliament was a positive development.

The new Parliament was a great improvement over the previous Legislative Council, although there were frequent demands for making the Cabinet accountable to it. It was felt that though it was a step in the right direction, it fell short of the popular demand for a truly democratic government. That step came with the promulgation of the 1952 Constitution, a step that was welcomed by the people and the political parties then in existence. A step, however, that was soon reversed under the terrific pressures of the political agitation and turmoil of the 1950s.

Between 1947 and 1967, nine parliaments were elected. The ninth parliament was prorogued several times before its final dissolution in 1975. The reason for lengthening its term was the occupation of the West Bank by Israel in 1967. It was felt that parliamentary elections could not be held while the West Bank was under occupation, and that any elections held on the East Bank alone would be tantamount to the final relinquishing of Jordan's claim of sovereignty over the area. However, it was felt that the burden of legislation, or at least some debate of Cabinet activity, if not the responsibility of that body to a quasi-representative body, was very much in need. Thus in 1978 a Consultative Council was appointed by the King from among certain of the country's notables and political personages. Many of the new members had not been in the public eye previously. Another innovation was the appointment of three prominent women to the council. The council, currently functioning, acts as a debating arena for government activities. Laws are submitted to it for consideration, and its debates are widely publicized in the mass media. It is no doubt short of a parliament and genuine representative democratic institutions, yet it is a step in the right direction until such time as elections can be held and a more relaxed atmosphere prevails.

Jordan is situated geographically at the heart of the Arab World. Because of the centrality of the Palestine problem and its importance and primacy for the entire Arab nation, it is thus once again in the heart of the Arab people. The frustration, anger and confusion described earlier in the form of a confession only touched on the bare outline and the surface of that sense of bewilderment. The 1920s saw the call for a constitutional, liberal, and parliamentary-type democracy in every Arab country. With the advent of the 1930s, an emphasis on socialism and social content to democratic institutions began to develop. The second-generation leadership was taken by contemporary ideology. Thus far, people and parties had vehemently opposed the presence of the colonial power, yet its institutions and ideas were not totally rejected. A reconciliation might still be possible.

The disappointment that took place following the termination of World War II was unparalleled in previous times. Israel mushroomed into the area overnight. The Western betrayal spoken of after World War I was complete. To ensure its constant hold on the area, the West planted Israel as a fortress outpost of its interests. Xenophobia and anti-Westernism, only a mild rash after World War I, now became a very serious virus penetrating and eating at the heart and soul of every Arab. Soon, certain political parties and ideologies "discovered" liberal democracy to be a "farce", another opiate of the masses designed to lull their senses and keep them in abject slavery and poverty. They also learned that class privileges and distinctions increased rather than decreased in such a system. Thus, the hatred of Western betrayal on the international level also turned inward to eat at the primordial and shaky-to-begin-with liberal institutions. Their doom was a matter of time.

Pan-Arabism, pan-Islamism, Communism, Nasserism, Ba'thism and others were ideologies that thrust themselves on the Arab political scene with force and intensity. This was the age of "isms", in Jordan and the rest of the Arab world. The word thrills and the wordy compositions of the leaders of these political movements; indeed, intellectual upheavals were like balm to the soul. Every Arab found himself a follower of this or that ideology, though intellectually, modern political ideologies might still have run ahead of true acceptance of them. In the same household one would often find a medley of debate between brothers holding different ideologies. It was believed that *Mahdi*, the *Messiah*, the Savior, must come through one of these ideologies.

Some ideologies attempted a wedding in time, delving into the past and hoping to apply what was retrieved to the present, which in turn would become a blueprint for the future. The *Salafiyyah*, following the ancestors, had its popular appeal; and it is still the most potent force in moving the masses. Some ideologies were more secular, though not denying the importance or primacy of religion as a factor in politics and life. Ba'thism, pan-Arab political movement developed at that time, still appeals to many. On the practical level, the Ba'th Party now controls Syria and Iraq. Communism, intellectually attractive to many, was always weak at the popular, grassroots, level. Then and now, it seems to have secured itself a niche from whence to preach its dogma. The Muslim Brethren, the Tahrir, or Liberation movement, both Islamic yet vying with each other for the soul and heart of the average man, also prevailed.

A full catalogue of political ideas and ideologies of this period following the creation of Israel would not be difficult to list. The point is that the relaxed, or semi-relaxed atmosphere of political development prior to 1948 seemed to have disappeared, never to return to any Arab country, including Jordan. Henceforth, and now in hindsight, no compromise would be tolerated. If you are not in agreement with me, you are either stupid or maybe a traitor. The word takes on such a hallow sanctity and the average man is collecting these nuggets of wisdom without heed. Charismatic leaders emerged who captured the hearts of the people. They expanded their mass media facilities, especially their radio stations. The Voice of Ahmad al-Said, a radio announcer from Cairo, was a dread to moderates and radicals alike who were at odds with Abdel Nasser; and each regime created its own Ahmad al-Said.

Layer upon layer of frustration was stacked. Many changes took place mostly accompanied by verbal violence. Many violent "revolutions" too, and always new hopes. Jordan, always considered the weakest link in the chain, stood in the midst of all this turmoil like a feather in the wind, and suffered the consequences. Again, and because of the centrality of the Palestine problem to Arab thinking and because of the presence of Palestinians in Jordan, this country became a mirror reflecting these mushrooming political ideologies and dogmas. It was not uncommon for a Jordanian then, and I suspect even now, to listen to several radio stations each morning, sampling the political vehemence and dipping his hands into each dish. These stations, pamphlets, leaflets, newspapers, utterances, all competed for his loyalty and often, at least intellectually, he belonged to more than one ideology, sometimes all, anything, anybody that would offer a glimmer of hope. Among four Jordanians there were more than four political ideologies! That was the scene, and Jordan was its mirror. The unity of thought , intellectual, political, social or on any other level that once existed in the Arab world, was no more. The replacement is still a bewildering array of ideas that cannot be easily described or analyzed. The best description is that ours is now an eclectic approach, choosing from both time and space, the heritage and the contemporary, and the end result is a new intellectual mosaic, a hybrid, often a wedding of anomalies.

With this scene it is sometimes difficult for me to see how Jordan survived at all. The fascinating thing is that through it all, Jordan attempted to maintain its parliamentary institutions and clung tenaciously to them as it still does. The realization that it cannot ignore the hurricane around, and often within, taught its leadership to exercise more and more control and power. Then and now, a Jordanian leader would retort: "How can you expect Jordan to be an island of democracy in a sea of tyranny?" It is a question not easy to answer, though easy to contemplate.

Because of the character of its leadership, King Abdullah Ibn al-Hussein (1921–1951), then King Hussein Ibn Talal (1952 to the present), Jordan maintained its basically moderate and Western orientation. The pressure of circum-stances, internal, regional and international, forced Jordan to waver, often erratically, between an authoritarian and a semi-democratic system. That is why it is very difficult to classify it under one typology or another. I often think it is somewhere in that twilight zone between an authoritarian patriarchal system and a liberal one. Yet, most observers and analysts, both local and from abroad, will readily admit it is one of the most responsive, efficient, merciful and comfortable regimes in the area. These observers will point out that though Jordan's political development has been arrested because of internal pressure and external circumstances, it has adopted a humane approach to its political difficulties. And it is to Jordan's credit that despite the difficult odds it has had to face, it has passionately avoided any resort to violence. Adversaries and opposition leaders have been treated, by-and-large, in a humane fashion; physical annihilation, assassination or murder have been completely avoided. One may wonder what the cost of this lack of political institutional development may be, though it is difficult to assess the effects just now. Maybe the time has now passed, and the deviation from the path can and will be righted.

The adversaries, in most cases, were rehabilitated and were reabsorbed into the system, many becoming ardent allies and supporters.

The Palestinian opposition leaders, though generally not altogether happy, will readily admit that under past and present circumstances, and considering the violence and bloodshed witnessed in the surrounding area, Jordan's performance has been better than expected. Many, whether Jordanian or Palestinian opposition leaders, will privately wish the regime all the goodwill in the world, though they feel it their duty to appear in opposition.

Is this weakness of the opposition or cleverness of the regime? It is a very difficult question to answer. Maybe the answer contains elements of both for, it is the mark of the times to be confused. Many honest men, in Jordan and elsewhere in the Arab world, commenced their political careers at one end of the political spectrum, swung to the opposite end, and then settled comfortably somewhere in the middle; an entire generation, to be counted by the hundreds or indeed by the thousands, swings in this way. Had it been only one man or a few, one could accuse them of intellectual dishonesty, perhaps even of opportunism. Yet, that was not the case. It was, as it perhaps still is, an uncertain generation drowned by colossal events and grabbing at anything that might offer solid and steady direction. In Jordan, the regime, personified by the King, offered that steady direction when everything else seemed to waver. You might have disagreed with Abdullah and Hussein, but you always saw them standing there, sure of themselves, or seemingly so, and you knew what they stood for.

Several factors account for the success of the Jordanian experiment in politics, an experiment that has withstood the often very cruel and severe frontal attacks of its adversaries, both local and regional. Among these is that both King Abdullah and now King Hussein have assumed an air of "bigness", grandness, about them. Often, they refused to retaliate in kind to venomous attacks against their person, style and regime. It was, as it still is, a mark of their "bigness" and strength that the very attacker will soon reconcile with them, exchange visits and forget the old enmity. King Hussein has undergone so many such turn-abouts in his lifetime it has become a feature of his conduct in policy. He has given the lesson of "bigness", that as a statesman he does not deal on the personal level, and that in politics there are no permanent friends or enemies, only interests.

King Hussein

King Hussein has become a legend in his own time. I was in a taxi going to the airport in Honolulu; the driver was a Korean who hardly spoke English. He exclaimed: "You are from Jordan … ah King Hussein … he is a good man!" This scene is familiar to the people of Jordan travelling abroad, whether in Europe, Asia or Africa. In a recent interview with the international edition of *al-Nahar* newspaper, the interviewer asked: "Your Majesty, a myth grows around you with the passage of time. You have been in power now for 27 years , you made of the weakest link in the Arab chain the strongest. What is the secret of your success?" In his reply, the King gave credit to the Lord who has guided his steps and to his people to whom he is honored to belong and to give service. His modesty attributing his success to the Lord and his people is correct only up to a point, for, the man himself has had something to do with it. The interviewer calls him the young dean of the Arab rulers. Why is that?

He is legitimate. He comes from a family whose honor and tradition cannot be questioned, and his right to govern, to reign and rule in the Arab tradition is not questioned. He did not jump to the throne, nor did he assume power by conspiracy. Both his immediate and distant ancestors are well known, and, as conceded by tradition, have the right to claim, exercise and hold power. Power and its exercise and manipulation come naturally to him. He has developed its exercise to the level of a profession. His latest book translated into Arabic has the title of Mihnati Ka Malik (My Profession as a King). In his chair, he may at times sit uneasily, but never illegitimately. If he were overthrown, he knows that no one would ever accuse him of having assumed power illegitimately in the first place. Psychologically, traditionally, and even religiously, power is not alien to him. As scion of one of the noblest houses of Arabia and Islam in medieval times, and heir to the Arab Revolt in this century, he has many claims on authority. And though *Uneasy Lies the Head*, as he entitled one of his books, that head knows the serenity of legitimacy and the exercise of governance.

Like his grandfather, King Abdullah, at whose hands he studied, he has a rare quality in rulers called in Arabic *al-Hilm*. It is a term that is difficult to translate into other languages for, in it are included the virtues of patience, political wisdom, perseverance, mercy, firmness, understanding, bigness and many other positive traits. This *hilm* has made the avoidance of the use of violence almost the hallmark of Jordan's political experience, often adhering to the Arabic dictum "mercy above justice". In Turkish there is a proverb that says a fish begins to rot first in its head. Similarly, it is believed that if the head holds some understanding, patience and mercy, these traits will soon permeate to the lower echelons of government. The King is often referred to by the more traditional-minded as *Sayyidnah*, our master, and in the Hashemite tradition, a term of endearment meaning the eldest in the family. He knows how to debate with his people, and has continued to do this in spite of all difficulties. In his speeches, which he addresses to the nation on frequent occasions, he refers to the people as "my Jordanian family". He has developed this notion into a political ideology of unusually fine proportions. The people expect the head of the family, the patriarch, the super chief, to be patient, to understand and to forgive. The debate goes on in this spirit, and with the passage of time less and less bitterness is directed against the regime. He has, perhaps unaware of it himself, developed this parochial approach to the point where people within Jordan and outside it identify this country and its every activity with him. His personality, his "father" image, has developed so strongly that some say it has resulted in a certain "quietism" in Jordan's politics. People trust him, know he is around; some may feel they are unable, or that it is futile to do anything anyway. Thus, a sense of fatalism develops. Others ask what will happen when he is no longer around?

Because of the "family" approach, people, though unaware of it, feel a certain sense of closeness and belonging. Persons who are unhappy or bereaved feel there are always avenues open to reach the men in charge, the ministers, prime minister, the crown prince or the King. This is encouraged, and the King, on state or private occasions, welcomes people asking for favors or to redress what they consider an unjust act against them. On some of these occasions, people greeting the King are seen slipping a piece of paper, a petition, into his hand, which he immediately slips into his pocket. He answers all of them, or directs that they all be answered. This practice, with much variation, is close to the Jordanian Arab mentality, and indeed gives the impression of a relaxed family atmosphere.

King Hussein has developed a certain sense, almost intuitive, concerning what may or may not work. Frequently he includes in his speeches the statement that his is his *Qadar*, his fate. This emphasis on fate is not, however, fatalism for almost always he seems to be ahead of events. Often, he tours the country, meeting with the people, speaking to them, having lunch with them, and shaking their hands. Not only the King, but the regime has acquired a certain characteristic of flexibility, both ideological and physical. King Hussein's understanding of his people's mentality has helped him to become a barometer that gauges their moods ahead of time, and to be prepared for what is to come. Needless to say, it has added further dimensions to his stature as a "father", an understanding and flexible "father" who shuns ideological or methodological rigidity. I often marvel at seeing proud men twice his age address him. Some may say, "you are like a father whose directions are needed ... please remember that you are big and that the big should envelope the smaller ..." This practical and pragmatic approach has been one of the most important factors behind the strength and versatility of the regime. He has developed the knack of preserving a sense of order while meeting people's needs.

Though he is not averse to compromise and is well known as a pragmatic and practical leader, he is, I believe, a nationalist of deep loyalties. If he compromises, it is not out of a sense of striking a bargain beneficial to himself only, but because he believes this is good for the cause he serves. He is willing to compromise, but only up to a point beyond which he will not go; he maintains a code of ethics and honor in the political sphere beyond which he will not pass.

As a myth and a legend in his lifetime, he is a man who believes in possibilities and anticipates them. Just think that though he is only 44 years old, he is one of the oldest rulers on earth. He is the oldest practicing ruler. Emperor Hirohito and Queen Elizabeth are reigning, but not ruling. Though young, he has "created" all the leadership of modern Jordan. In the absence of political liberal institutions, parties, parliament and leadership must be personally chosen by him, or at least approved by him. Whether in the army, the Cabinet, the diplomatic corps or other top leadership positions, people are either hand-picked or approved by him. In this, he strikes and maintains a balance between the old and the new, the traditional and the modern. He does this with grace and determination all at the same time. All feel obligated and beholden to him. He has a quiet charisma, and when people are talking to him, he gives the impression that he is listening with his ears, nose, hair and every other part of his body. He captivates his audience with his listening, quiet, almost serene, and often melancholy smile. People admire how he keeps trying. Though he often sounds like the leader of the chorus in a Greek tragedy who keeps repeating his lines, people rarely tire of listening. Perhaps because of the size and resources of Jordan, he has avoided frontal attacks. Instead, he develops with understanding and patience, and has developed the strength and resilience of water, which envelopes and proves itself the strongest of all elements. It is true that age does not always bring wisdom. In some it only brings rigid arrogance. This is not the case with King Hussein, who has learned the wisdom of questioning the apparent reality and the ability to understand the questions, which is often more important than having ready answers.

Under his leadership, the modern Jordanian government has matured. Not only has it learned how to refrain from doing evil whenever possible; it has learned how to do good. Socially and economically, the country has developed beyond most expectations, considering its meager resources and the heavy burden it had to shoulder following several waves of forced immigration of destitute Palestinian refugees. Only in the political sphere has its attempt at institutionalization been stunted or retarded. Yet even here, the experiment is far from complete, and given time, a truly genuine democratic system may still emerge. King Hussein is a study in politics all by himself, for, he has developed survival into an art, and has shown that a strong man is often strongest alone. He gives the feeling that he can handle any situation.

This is more obvious since Jordan has had to live in adversity for most of its existence. Disorder always seems as if it is here to stay. Though strong and "from the throne", he makes true the statement that though people are subordinate to government, the ruled influence the ruler. Jordan's experience has been such an interaction. At times more intense than at others, it has shown that there are limits to the use of force, which can often destroy its frequent user, and that judging its limit is an art. The Shah of Iran and many others like him did not learn these limits. If King Hussein's role seems to be overemphasized, it deserves the emphasis, for he has developed into the fine mover and, at the same time, the medium of Jordanian political life. His outreach into world affairs has not been confined to the political area alone. Witness the open-mindedness towards developments in the socio-economic, medical, educational and research fields, the two universities, Hussein Medical City, the Royal Scientific Society and many other such institutions. Many of these functions and innovations he resolves, or encourages his younger brother, Crown Prince Hassan, to adopt.

Though Jordan is not a Western-style democracy, with political parties banned since 1957, there is an air of open mindedness and frankness not found elsewhere in the region. The debate that one witnesses on a variety of issues ranging from economic to the social and often the political is encouraged. The level of tolerance of the regime remains responsible and comparatively high, and the state has avoided the use of organized terror with admirable tenacity.

Crown Prince Al-Hassan Ibn Talal

On the domestic scene, the role played by Prince Hassan has been a dominant and invigorating one. In many senses, he plays the role described by the famous British constitutionalist Walter Bagehot in discussing the role of the British monarch: to give advice, consent and to educate. This is especially true since he has ready access at all times to the King, the prime minister, the various ministers, department heads, officers and public or private leaders in almost every walk of life. The role is further enhanced and strengthened since he enjoys the respect and confidence of the King. It is noticed, for instance, that he attends all important discussions or negotiations the King holds with foreign dignitaries and heads of state. His opinion is not only solicited in these matters, it is often critical.

Since 1966, the Prince, under the patronage of his brother King Hussein, has played a very important role in the development of the country. The King, obviously an excellent mentor, has encouraged the Prince to direct most of his energies to solving the country's socio-economic problems. The vigor with which he has taken to the task has become a by-word to planners and executives, not only in Jordan but in the Arab world as well. Indeed, the Prince quickly absorbed and assessed the situation, and then set himself to the task. In time, he began to move things, always and ever so gently, careful of the sensibilities and sensitivities of the people involved, whether lay or official. Frequently he will caution against what he calls *al-Khandaqah*, the penchant of executives and bureaucrats to jealously guard their prerogatives and jurisdictions. He takes a universal look at Jordan's problems, and is constantly at pains to integrate not only the problems but also the suggested solutions and follow-up.

Rarely has a monarchy been blessed with two such dedicated and hardworking leaders. It seems that Prince Hassan has learned from both his grandfather, King Abdullah, and his brother, King Hussein, the quality of *Hilm*. He never seems confused or lost. Under strenuous and often unfamiliar circumstances, he maintains his cool-headedness and nerve. Though young, he has developed both sight and vision, and is not only an interested party but the initiator of very innovative ideas as well. He has the capability of grasping a good idea, sponsoring and then executing it.

His powers are both constitutional, as Crown Prince, and extra-constitutional, as a key political personality. Many people look to him as a modern-day grand chief. In fact, many people consider him as a last resort to alleviate an injustice, redress a mistake, give justice to the weak, a sort of Jordanian *ombudsman*. He does all these tasks with firm gentleness, sympathy and understanding to all parties. Frequently, he takes the time to visit schools, hospitals, army bases, refugee camps, Bedouin villages and rural areas. People are rarely awed by him, for they consider him their own; they talk to him freely, airing their grievances, demanding redress and sometimes favors and jobs.

The people think of him as a good and steady influence, and admire his tenacity in his repeated attempts at solving Jordan's problems. They also admire the fact that he has become a helping hand to his brother.

Since 1966, he has promoted the formulation and implementation of the Jordanian Three Year (1973–1975) and Five Year (1976–1980) social and economic Development Plans. In this capacity, he earned a local and international reputation for being a dedicated and honest leader. So much has his international reputation expanded that he is intermittently asked to sponsor a conference in London, Paris, Washington, Geneva, Buenos Aires or other places. In his determination to expand Jordan's horizons, he has learned its problems and become its international ambassador to high-level conferences on transfer of technology, labor and the empowerment of women, and high-level conferences on finance, energy and other matters. His is a dialogue with the world on behalf of Jordan and often the Arab world. He buys new ideas and is good at selling them, too. Often, he comes in only when there are problems. Though constrained by not being part of government, he has developed his power to initiate, advise and consent.

Considerations

The only danger signal is that political institutions have lagged behind those in the socio-economic field. While this can be excused under the circumstances, it is not in the country's interest for this trend to continue. It is heartening, however, that the regime seems to be aware of this and has taken a step in the right direction through the establishment of the Consultative Council. Many believe that bolder steps should be taken when the time is right. It is just not healthy that a people with a cause like ours, always under the danger of being attacked, maintain the present quietism. One may find reasons and excuses, but I believe an opening-up will be welcomed and will be received with responsibility. Jordanians and Palestinians, I believe, have outgrown the political adolescence of the 1950s. This, in spite of my belief that we are still not capable of keeping a steady commitment to modern ideology, nor do we seem capable, just yet, of reconciling it with our private or public life. Reason is the strength of our personal familial and tribal loyalties that are slowly being ameliorated yet still maintain a hold. Nor should it be forgotten that it is in our tradition to look for the man, the person, the hero, and not the ideology or the institution.

The intellectual atmosphere, the level of education and our stage of socio-economic development necessitate that positive developments in the political sphere take place. The seemingly cool ashes of the present may be deceitful, and the political life must not continue to take the shape of who wins as the *Naqib*, president, of the medical, engineering, pharmaceutical and lawyers' associations. If anything, the elections of these associations have proved too divisive and bitter, with sectarian or provincial interests in them too prominent. Nor should political life continue in the form of the camouflaged or overt gossip at gatherings, funerals or in salons. It leaves the field wide open for the second-rate and the mediocre who have influence, money or a "loudmouth". The *Mustawzirin*, those who hope to become Cabinet ministers, though some may be deserving, should not be allowed to continue to dominate the field of Jordan's political life.

Jordan's evolutionary development, though halted temporarily, should, and I believe it will, continue on the path first outlined by King Abdullah and paved and widened by his grandson King Hussein. A path of open-minded, easy-going, relaxed and humane development towards a more participatory democratic and responsible system.

The Jordan Valley north of Lake Galilee. Weekly market, approx 1920–33.
G. Eric and Edith Matson, American Colony (Jerusalem).
Photo Department. Library of Congress.
Restoration by Kelvin Bown. *Reawakening the Past*, 2015.

Epilogue

Aristotle once remarked that only two things in life are constant: time and change. There is always time, and its dimension is all-enveloping. No one can escape the time dimension, ignore it, or live outside it. So, it is with change and living things; the moment they have life, change beings. Societies are also ever-changing, though the change is sometimes imperceptible. In history, we speak of the Umayyad, Abbasid, Ayyubid, Mamluk or Ottoman periods. Each era was different from the other, not just in the way of governance but in its style of life and its ways. In modern times change continues, yet it is not change that we speak of; rather, it is "changing". That is the will, the self-conscious will and desire to induce change rather than simply letting it happen. And here is where the will of the leader, ruler, preacher, decision-maker, government and state is most manifest. Ataturk was right: either change or be reduced to a life of enslavement. That is why all governments in the developing world are inducing change.

Amman, known as Rabath Ammon in Biblical times, and Philadelphia in the Roman period, and now representative of urbanization in Jordan, has changed. Until 1948, it was a rather sleepy little town of no more than 30,000 inhabitants; yet once change commenced, it was impossible to arrest or harness it. How did change begin, and where and why? Was it first in the military, the cultural or the socio-economic and political fields? Does not a Bedouin or a villager change immediately upon entering the city? Can the process be reversed or halted? What is the period of gestation before a new idea or tool takes hold?

The human history of the region has bequeathed legacies of tradition and ways of life one upon the other. One can even physically observe that from the shards found on or near a tel, and in the layers of earth and ashes at an archeological site. Religion, and now government, impose upon these layers a new pattern which is progressively modifying them. New values, tools, traditions, and ways are currently being superimposed, and even those whose lives are most comfortable in the grip of tradition are changing. Values change with the changing of the goals of a society. Today's Jordanian society, like most, if not all contemporary societies, is directed towards the common man, not the privileged few. Jordan, too, recognizes that the new order of things is not simply a negative one. Societies are like individuals, children of their time, and the present is the era of the welfare state. It is an uncertain, confusing, and bewildering one. Men and leaders live in more than one world at the same time. No one any longer has the answer ready at hand for every question. For, change once begun may out-distance individual and institutional development.

Ours, that is our Jordanian Arab society, is a "middling" one: an intermediate in the dimensions of both time and space. It is a historical link between the civilizations of antiquity and modernity, and it is a spatial link between the several existing cultures and societies of today. Jordan is in the heart of this intermediate civilization in terms of both time and space.

Can anyone describe a nation's moods and activities? Such an attempt is difficult when describing a single person. It is near impossible with a rich and complex social order. These essays were never meant to be a detailed catalogue of the life and activities of our people. I never attempted a complete feast; only the hors d'œuvre. Indeed, it is only a morsel to whet the appetite and to generate interest and discussion. Prudence, if not economy and modesty, demand these remarks for, indeed, how can one describe all the agony and pain of change, the tension, rootlessness, the groping for firmer ground, firmer beliefs and ideas? Our land, Jordan, is not only starved for water, it is also starved for a firm and steady grip on life, not that we are worse off than the other cultures and societies which we use as models. There, too, the ground is shaky and often erupting in a variety of patterns of psychedelic, ever-changing effects.

Our internal difficulties have been compounded by the external challenge posed by Israel. It has added to our frustration and confusion, brought to us by that cold and merciless Western wind, a wind from which we have suffered since the Crusades. It shall, one day, face our gathering storm.

Appendix

Jordan: The East Bank in figures

1952 – 1979 – 2020

	1952	1979	2020
Population	587,193	2,152,273	10,806,000
% Urban Population[1]	31	65.8	92
Birth rate	0.047	0.05	0.0017
Death rate	0.021	0.012	0.003
% Labor force working in agriculture[2]	35	18	1.7[3]
% Labor force working in services	44	63	82
% Labor force working in industry, mining, and construction	21	19	16.3
Illiteracy rate[4]	70.0%	29.3%	1.8%
Illiteracy rate males	–	17.8%	1.4%
Illiteracy rate females	–	40.9%	2.2%
Students	139,670[5]	698,205	2,151,670
Students males	103,189	379,837	1,087,476

	1952	1979	2020
Students females	36,481	318,368	1,064,194
Ratio of female students to total enrolment	26.1%	45.6%	49.5%
Ratio of total enrolment to population	10.5%	32.4%	19%
Ratio of females students to population	2.7%	14.8%	9.8%
Teachers	1,184	25,855	140,248
Teachers males	1,135	12,772	42,034
Teachers females	49	13,083	98,214
Students per teacher	41	27	15
Females in universities	22	3,959	163,778
College students abroad	2,861[6]	45,000	7,202
Schools	360	2,584	7,551
Vocational schools and centers	2	33	–
Teachers institutions	–	11	–
Establishments (employing 5 or more)	98	1,520	17,181
Banks (with branches)	3	106	861
Physicians	97	1,893	23[7]
Pharmacists	49	515	11.9[8]
Hospitals	–	35	116
Hospital beds	623	3,738	14[9]
Clinics	46	346	1,194

	1952	1979	2020
Cars	7,683	106,919[10]	1,729,343
Radio per thousand	39[11]	203[12]	–
Television per thousand	–	128[13]	–
Telephones per thousand	5	20.9	–
Tourists (Foreign arrivals)	2,775	1,213,381	5,203,600
Agricultural land[14] (Dunum)[15]	3,441,626	3,612,816	2,818,958[16]
Fallow for rest	–	834,688	760,653
Area planted grains (Dunum)	3,253,457	2,113,617	718,375
% of area planted grains	94.5%	73.5%	25%
Area planted vegetables	137,368	301,046	248,984
% of area planted vegetables	4%	10.4%	8.8%
Area planted fruits (Dunum)	1,9164	414,789	780,634
% of area planted fruits	0.6%	14.4%	27.7%
Area planted tobacco (Dunum)	31,637	44,400	0
% of area planted tobacco	0.9%	1.5%	0%
Forest trees (Dunum)	274,785	544,000	980,000
Livestock	245,069	1,288,700	3,157,700[17]
Imports (mill. Dinars)[18]	14.2	565[19]	12,077

	1952	1979	2020
Exports (mill. Dinars)	1.5	80[20]	5,044.4
Government revenues in (mill. Dinars)	32.3	493.7	7,028.9
Foreign aid (mill. Dinars)	6.3	225.2	790.8[21]
Ratio of aid to revenue	27%	45.6%	11.25%
Expenditures (mill. Dinars)	20.8	513.6	9,211.3
Gross National Product (mill. Dinars)	45	791.9	31,025
Per capita income (Dinar)	35	367.9	2871.1

1. 10,000 and more.
2. Figures on Labor in Column I are for 1961 while those in column II are for 1975.
3. Numbers only include Jordanian workers.
4. Figures on illiteracy in column II are for 1976.
5. The figure includes the West Bank
6. This figure was for the academic year 1955/1956.
7. For Column III, data from the Ministry of Health is per 10,000 individuals.
8. For Column III, data from the Ministry of Health is per 10,000 individuals.
9. For Column III, data from the Ministry of Health is per 10,000 individuals.
10. This figure was for the middle of 1979.
11. For the year 1957.
12. For the year 1972.
13. For the year 1975.
14. All the figures in Column II on agriculture are for the year 1978.
15. A Dunum is approximately ¼ of an acre.
16. For Column III, all figures on agriculture are from the Agriculture Census of 2017 by the Department of Statistics.
17. For 2019.

18. A Dinar is about 3.3 U.S. Dollars (before 1989)
19. Estimate is based on information for the first ten months of 1979.
20. Estimate is based on information for the first ten months of 1979.
21. Foreign aid only includes direct budget aid.

Selected Bibliography

Al-Abbadi, A.O., *Min al Qiyam wa al-Adab al-Badawiyyah*, Amman, Wakalat al-Sahafah al-Urduniyyah, 1976

Abd Al-Nasser, Gamal, *Falsafat al-Thawrah* (The Philosophy of the Revolution), Cairo, 1954

Abdullah, King of Jordan, *Memoirs of King Abdullah of Trans-Jordan* (Translated by G.Khoury, edited by P. Graves). New York: Philosophical Library, 1950.

Abdullah, King of Jordan, *My Memoirs Completed*, by Harold Gliden, Washington, D.C. American Council of Learned Societies, 1954.

al-'Abidi, Mahmoud, *Ajanib Fi Diyarinah*, (Foreigners In Our Land), Amman, al-Matabi' al-Ta'awuniyyah, 1974.

Abidi, Aqil Haydar Hasan, *Jordan: A Political Study*, New York, Asia Publishing House, 1965.

Abu Hassan, M., *Turath al-Badu al-Qada'i*, (Bedouin Judicial Heritage), Amman, Manshourat Dar al-Thaqafah Wa al-Funun, 1974.

Abu Jaber, Kamel, *The Arab Ba'ath Party*, Syracuse University Press, 1966.

Abu Jaber, Kamel et.al., *The Bedouins of Jordan: A People in Transition*, Royal Scientific Society, 1978. Photographs by Rami Khouri

Abu Jaber, Shabeeb, al-Mujtama' al-Urduni, (The Jordanian Society), Amman, al-Sharikah al-Arabiyyah li at-Tiba'ah wa al-Nasher, 1979.

Antonius, George, *The Arab Awakening*. 3rd. Ed. New York, Capricorn Books, 1965.

Aruri, Nasser H., *Jordan: A Study in Political Development (1921-1965)*, The Hague, Martinus Nyhoff, 1972.

Awad, Mohamed, *Living Conditions of Nomadic, Semi Nomadic, and Settled Tribal Groups*, Pages 135-184 in Abdullah M. Lutfiyya and Charles W. Churchill (eds), *Readings in Arab Middle Eastern Societies and Cultures*, The Hague, Mouton, 1970.

Berger, Morroe, *The Arab World Today*, New York, Doubleday, 1962.

Berger, Rabbi Elmer, *Who Knows Better Must Say So*, New York, American Council of Judaism, 1955.

Brokelmann, Carl., *History of the Islamic Peoples*, New York, Putnam, 1947.

Buhairi, S., *Goghrafiyyat al Urdun*, (The Geography of Jordan), Amman, al-Sharq Press, 1973.

Burckhardt, J.L., *Travels in Arabia*, 2 vols, London, John Murray, 1829.

Coon, Carleton S., *Caravan: The Story of the Middle East*, London, Jonathan Cope, 1952.

Davis, Helen Miller, *Constitutions, Electoral Laws, Treaties of States in the Near and Middle East*, 2d. Ed., Durham, N.C., Duke University Press, 1953.

Dearden, Ann, *Jordan*, London, Robert Hale, 1958.

Diqs, Isaac, *A Bedouin Boyhood*, London, Allen and Unwin, 1967.

The Economic Development of Jordan, Baltimore. Published for the International Bank for Reconstruction and Development, the Johns Hopkins Press, 1957.

Edmonds, C.J., *Kurds, and Arabs*, London, Oxford University Press, 1957.

Fisher, Sydney N., ed., *Social Forces in the Middle East*, Ithaca, N.Y., Cornell University Press, 1955.

Fisher, Sydney N., *The Middle East: A History*, New York, Knopf, 1959.

Fistere, J. And I., *Jordan, The Holy Land*, Beirut, Middle East Export Press, N.D.

Ghawanmeh, Yusuf, D., *Amman Hadaratuhah Wa Tarikhuhah*, (Amman, History and Civilization), Amman, Dar al-Liwa, 1979.

H.A.R. Gibb, et al. (Eds.), Badw. *The Encyclopedia of Islam*, London, Luzac, pages 872-892, 1960.

Glubb, John Bagot, *Peace in the Holy Land*, London, Hodder and Stoughton, 1971.

Glubb, John B., *A Soldier With the Arabs*, London, Hodder and Stoughton, 1959.

Glubb, John B., *The Story of the Arab Legion*, London, Hodder and Stoughton, 1948.

Halpern, Manfred, *The Politics of Social Change in the Middle East and North Africa*, Princeton, Princeton University Press, 1965.

Harris, George L., *Jordan: Its People, its Society, its Culture*, New York, Grove Press, 1958.

Hitti, Philip, K., *The Arabs: A Short History*, Princeton, Princeton University Press, 1943.

Hitti, Philip, *History of the Arabs*, New York, Macmillan, 1968.

Hourani, Albert H., *Minorities in the Arab World*, New York, Oxford University Press, 1947.

Hourani, Albert H., *Syria and Lebanon*, New York, Oxford University Press, 1946.

Hurewitz, J.C., *Middle East Dilemmas*, New York, Harper, 1953.

Hurewitz, J.C., *Middle East Politics: The Military Dimension*, New York, Praeger, 1969.

Hussein, King of Jordan, *Uneasy Lies the Head*, London, Bernard Geis, 1962.

Hussein, King of Jordan, *Mihnati Ka Malik*, (My Profession as a King), Trans. From French, Amman, Matabi, al-Sharikah al-Arabiyyah Li al-Tiba'ah wa al-Nashr, 1978.

al-Kailani, Faruq, *Istiqlal al-Qada*, (The Independence of the Judiciary), Cairo, Dar al-Nahdah al-Arabiyyah, 1977.

al-Kailani, Faruq, *Shar'iat-Asha'ir Fi al-Watan al-Arabi*, (Tribal Law in the Arab Fatherland), Beirut, Dar al-Ilm Lil-Malayin, 1972.

Kerr, Malcolm, *The Arab Cold War*, New York, Oxford University Press, 1967.

Khouri, Fred J., *The Arab Israeli Dilemma*, Syracuse, Syracuse University Press, 1968.

Kirkbride, Alec, *A Crackle of Thorns: Experience in the Middle East*, London: John Murray, 1965.

Laqueur, Walter Z., ed. *The Middle East in Transition*, London, Routledge and Kegan Paul, 1958.

Lawrence, Thomas E., *Seven Pillars of Wisdom*, London, J. Cope, 1935.

Lenczowski, George, *The Middle East in World Affairs*, Ithaca, N.Y., Cornell University Press, 1956.

Lerner, Daniel, *The Passing of Traditional Society; Modernizing the Middle East*, Glencoe, Free Press, 1958.

Lilienthal Alfred, *Other Side of the Coin*, New York, Devin-Adair, 1965.

Longrigg, Stephen, *The Middle East*, Chicago, Aldine, 1963.

Al-Madi, Munib, and Musa, Suleiman, *Tarikh al-Urdun Fi al-Qarn al-'Ishrin*, (History of Jordan in the Twentieth Century), Amman, N.D.

Mahafzah, Ali, *'Ahd al-Amarah*, (The Emirate Era), Amman, Matba'at al-Quwwat al-Musalahah, 1973.

Mahafzah, Ali, *al-Itijahat al-Fikriyyah 'Ind al-'Arab*, (Intellectual Trends Among the Arabs), Beirut, al-Ahliyyah Li al-Tawzi' wa al-Nashr, 1975.

al-Marayati, Abid, A., *Middle Eastern Constitutions and Electoral Laws*, New York, Prager, 1968.

Mazur, Michael, *Economic Development in Jordan*, Chapter 5 in Charles A. Cooper and Sidney S. Alexander (eds.), *Economic*

Development and Population Growth in the Middle East, New York, American Elsevier, 1972.

Ministry of Culture and Information, *Al-Urdun Fi Khamsin 'Aman*, 1921–1971, (Jordan in Fifty Years, 1921–1971), Amman, 1972.

Musa, Suleiman, *Gharbiyun Fi Bilad al-'Arab*, (Westerners In Arabian Lands), Ministry of Culture and Information Publications, 1969.

Musa, Suleiman, *Ta'sis al-Amarah al-Urduniyyah*, (The Establishment of the Emirate of Jordan), Amman, Al-Matba'ah al-Urduniyyah, 1971.

Nuseibeh, Hazem Zaki, *The Ideas of Arab Nationalism*, Ithaca, N.Y., Cornell University Press, 1956.

Patai, R., *The Hashemite Kingdom of Jordan*, Princeton, Princeton University Press, 1958.

Peake, F.G., *A History of Jordan and its Tribes*, 2 vols. Florida, Coral Gables, 1958.

al-Rabay'ah, A.H., *al-Mujtama' al-Badawi al-Urduni*, (The Bedouin Society of Jordan), Amman, al-Matabi' al-Ta'awuniyyah, 1974.

Rivlin, J. and Szyliowicz, eds., *The Contemporary Middle East: Tradition and Innovation*, New York, Random House, 1965.

Sharabi, Hisham, *Government and Politics of the Middle East in the Twentieth Century*, Princeton, Van Nostrand, 1962.

Sharabi, Hisham, *Maqadamah Li Dirasat al-Mujtama' al-Arabi*, (Introduction to the Study of Arab Society), Beirut, al-Dar al-Muttahidah li al-Nashr, 1975.

Sharayhah, Wadi, *Al-Tanmiyiah Al-Iqtisadiyyiah Fi Al-Urdun*, (Economic Development in Jordan), Cairo, Mutba'at al Nahdah al-Jadidah, 1968.

Shwadran, Benjamin, *Jordan: A State of Tension*, New York, Council for Middle Eastern Affair Press, 1959.

Sparrow, Gerald, *Hussein of Jordan*, London, George Harrap Co. Ltd, 1960.

Thompson, J.H. and Reischauer, R.D., *Modernization of the Arab World*, New York, Nostrand, 1966.

Tuqan, Baha'-Uddin, *A Short History of Jordan*, London, Luzac, 1945.

Tuqan, Fawwaz, *Al-Ha'ir, Bahth Fi al-Qusur al-Ammawiyyah Fi al-Badiyyah*, (al-Ha'ir, Study of Ummayyad Castles in the Desert), Amman, Ministry of Culture Publications, 1979.

Votikiotis, P.J., *Politics and the Military in Jordan, A Study of the Arab Legion*, 1921-57, New York, Praeger, 1967.

Weir, Shelagh, *The Bedouin*, London, The World of Islam Publishing Co., 1976.

About the Author

Dr. Kamel S. Abu Jaber (1932–2020) received his PhD from Syracuse University and did a postdoctoral programme in Oriental studies at Princeton University.

Following an academic career in the United States, he returned to Jordan to pursue an extensive academic career as Professor of Political Science and Dean of the College of Economics & Commerce at the University of Jordan. He also assumed a political career becoming Minister of Economy in 1973, Minister of Foreign Affairs in 1991, heading the joint Jordanian-Palestinian delegation to the Madrid Peace Conference. He also served as Senator in the Jordanian Parliament. Other positions include: Director, Jordan University's Center for Strategic Studies; Director, Queen Alia Social Welfare Fund; President, the Jordanian Institute of Diplomacy; President, Higher Council for Media; President, Royal Institute for Interfaith Studies; President, Jordan Institute for Middle Eastern Studies.

Dr. Kamel S. Abu Jaber has written many articles and books, among them *The Arab Ba'ath Socialist Party* (1966), *The Palestinians: People of the Olive Tree* (1993) and *Sheepland* (2005).